∞

Christian Self-Mastery

Basil W. Maturin

Christian Self-Mastery

How to Govern Your Thoughts,
Discipline Your Will, and
Achieve Balance in Your Spiritual Life

SOPHIA INSTITUTE PRESS®
Manchester, New Hampshire

Christian Self-Mastery is an abridged edition of *Self-Knowledge and Self-Discipline* (Paterson, New Jersey: St. Anthony Guild Press, 1939) and includes minor revisions to the original text.

Printed in the United States of America

Jacket design by Lorraine Bilodeau

On the jacket: "Profile of a Man Praying,"
SW Productions/PhotoDisc.

Sophia Institute Press®
Box 5284, Manchester, NH 03108
1-800-888-9344
www.sophiainstitute.com

Nihil obstat: C. Schut, D.D., *Censor Deputatus*
Imprimatur: Edm. Can. Surmont, *Vicarius Generalis*
Westminster, October 28, 1915

Library of Congress Cataloging-in-Publication Data

Maturin, B. W. (Basil William), 1847-1915.
Christian self-mastery : how to govern your thoughts, discipline your will, and achieve balance in your spiritual life / Basil W. Maturin.
— Abridged ed.
    p.   cm.
Rev. ed. of: Self-knowledge and self-discipline. 1939.
Includes bibliographical references.
ISBN 1-928832-21-0 (pbk. : alk. paper)
    1. Christian life — Catholic authors. 2. Spiritual life — Catholic Church. I. Maturin, B. W. (Basil William), 1847-1915. Self-knowledge and self-discipline. II. Title.

BV4501.2.M387 2001
248.4'82 — dc21   2001020102

01 02 03 04 05 06 07 10 9 8 7 6 5 4 3 2 1

∞

Contents

Editor's note: The biblical quotations in the following pages are taken from the Douay-Rheims edition of the Old and New Testaments. Where applicable, biblical quotations have been cross-referenced with the differing names and enumeration in the Revised Standard Version, using the following symbol: (RSV =).

∞

Christian Self-Mastery

Chapter One

∽∽

Develop self-knowledge

∞

There are two spheres of knowledge in which everyone who is endeavoring after any growth in the spiritual life must be making some advance: the knowledge of God and the knowledge of self. We can all readily perceive the necessity of growth in the knowledge of God as essential to any development of the spiritual life. The connection is obvious. "This," said our Lord, "is eternal life, that they may know Thee, the only true God, and Jesus Christ whom Thou hast sent."[1]

A certain moral sympathy is absolutely necessary as a condition of friendship, and holiness consists in friendship with God. If we would be in any sense the friends of God, we must have at least that desire for holiness without which such friendship would be impossible; the growth in the knowledge of God is the deepening of this friendship. "If we say that we have fellowship with Him and walk in darkness, we lie, and do not the truth."[2]

But the knowledge of self is as necessary for the spiritual life as is the knowledge of God. It is at once a condition and an

[1] John 17:3.
[2] 1 John 1:6.

effect of this knowledge. The more we grow in the knowledge of God, the deeper our knowledge of self, and if we would attain to any knowledge of God, there must be some knowledge of self. When Isaiah saw the Lord's glory in the Temple, there was at once a deepening sense of his own sinfulness: "Woe is me . . . because I am a man of unclean lips . . . and I have seen with my eyes the King, the Lord of hosts."[3] For the soul is created in the image of God, and it cannot approach His presence without perceiving how unlike it is to Him in whose image it was made.

To know God is to know self. To have no knowledge of God is to walk in darkness, to have no absolute standard by which to gauge and measure yourself. Those who shut God altogether out of their lives are able to live in stupid if not happy ignorance of what failures their lives are.

∞

We do not really know ourselves

Yet there are few things more surprising, when we come to think of it, than our ignorance of ourselves. It is more than ignorance, for ignorance means only failure in knowledge, but we go beyond that: not only are many of us ignorant of a great part of our own character, but we often imagine ourselves to be quite different from what we are. It would seem almost impossible that it should be so, if we did not know it to be only too true.

How is it possible for a man to close his eyes to the most patent and pressing facts connected with himself, involving

---

[3]   Isa. 6:5.

the gravest consequences, which are perfectly evident to everyone except himself? We are often amused by hearing others give their opinion of themselves and their gifts and powers. We are amused — sometimes amazed — that their estimate is so utterly different from what those who have only a very slight knowledge of them can see at a glance to be the true one. We hear people boast of gifts that everyone but themselves knows they do not possess. On the other hand, we see men of great powers and influence tormented with an almost morbidly low estimate of their own capacity.

Yet we do not consider that perhaps we are as completely mistaken in our judgment of ourselves. Most of us have at some time been accused of some fault in our character that we repudiated at the time with indignation begotten of the sincere conviction that the accusation was untrue, and yet perhaps years afterward we found ourselves mistaken and that the criticism was correct. How is it possible that such a thing should be?

Listen to two friends discussing and criticizing one another. What is more common than the tone of protest or repudiation with which some fault or some virtue is discussed? Yet do we not feel naturally inclined to say, "Surely the man must know himself better than his friend can know him. If he says he hasn't that gift or fault, who can know whether he has or not better than he?" We do not say this aloud, because experience has proven to us how often the critic is right, and that in many cases a man is the worst judge of himself.

Indeed we may have a very deep knowledge of human character in general, and yet be profoundly ignorant of our own character. We look with the same eyes, yet the eyes that pierce so easily through the artifices and deceptions of others become clouded and the vision becomes disturbed when they turn inward and examine self. Moreover, it is to be remembered that self-knowledge has nothing to do with mere cleverness or intellectual insight, but is largely, if not entirely, moral.

When we consider how intensely self-conscious is the age in which we live, and the amount of time most people spend on themselves in one way or another, what an absorbingly interesting study is that of the human heart, and all the more interesting when it is our own. We are amazed that most of us are nevertheless so lacking in self-knowledge that very often our latest acquaintance could tell us things about ourselves that we would refuse to believe — yet they are undoubtedly true.

∞

We don't know what keeps us from God

No sooner do we become thoughtful and begin to pray and try to get near God than all this comes upon us with an overwhelming sense of incapacity. How are we to advance? What are we to struggle with? Deep shadows are seen to lie across the soul, but we cannot tell what casts them. We feel held back from God, but we cannot grasp and bring to light what it is that holds us back.

We know well, indeed, some one or two prominent sins that have dogged our life's path for years, and against these we struggle bravely and are conscious that God is helping us. But of these we are now scarcely afraid; such faults are visible, tangible, in a sense healthy, inasmuch as they can be met and fought face-to-face.

No, it is the unseen, the impalpable, the mysterious, that paralyzes even the strongest men, and to these the soul has now awakened. There are ghostly fears that flit about the background of the soul, stirring up evil, suggesting all kinds of doubts and fears. We hear the silent footsteps of unseen foes hurrying here and there. We find ourselves at times excited by an unreasonable antagonism to the God whom, with all our reason and all our hearts, we long to cling to and to serve.

At other times the heart is wrung dry of every emotion, every serious thought is chased from the brain, until, kneeling before God with silent lips and dull, vacant mind, we feel almost hopeless. "If I only knew what it is that holds me back, if I could only see the enemy, I would not fear to fight him, but I now begin to realize that there is a life within of which I know nothing, that my mind has formed, habits have grown, and strangers have entered and taken possession of my heart, and I know them not, neither their nature nor their name."

The soul on awakening to God wakens to the sense of its ignorance of itself and the impossibility of making any decided advance without self-knowledge. It is at such moments haunted with the thought of the possibility of having been insincere in Confession, or that there is some unforgiven sin binding it to earth. At other moments it fears delusion, fears that it has never really repented and that the prayers and Communions that seemed earnest were the mere result of emotional excitement.

Verily, it is possible to imagine anything when we find ourselves the victim of effects traceable to no known cause, on first awakening to the fact that we are practically a stranger to ourselves — a stranger, that is to say, to a whole inner world of motive, of complex aims and wily thoughts that slip off into the darkness as we try to turn upon them the light of conscience, leaving us with a deepening sense of alarm and restlessness. We are surprised and shocked when, as sometimes happens, we find some strong motive or passion or ambition standing like a draped form whose expression we cannot catch, in the very council chamber of the soul, arguing with the reason or threatening the conscience or stimulating the imagination to take its side and plead its cause. It stands there with the ease and bearing of an honored counselor whose words are wont to have weight, and its voice is as of one in authority. But when we strive to grasp and unveil it, so that we may detect its origin, the voice is suddenly hushed into silence and is gone.

We are awakened to the knowledge that motives sway us that we cannot analyze, yet which seem to have gained position and power long ago, even though we have only now become conscious of their existence.

It is only in moments of retirement or of prayer, when the soul is hushed in silence and we pass in spirit through its various chambers and corridors, that, if we suddenly find ourselves face-to-face with such a presence, we are able to recognize its nature, and at once trace many of our gravest failures to its agency. "Where did it come from?" we ask ourselves. "How long has it been there? How did it gain admittance?" That pride that somehow found entrance into the heart and set itself to watch and manipulate our thoughts at their very source: we have seen it now for the first time face-to-face, and it has been like a revelation. It has explained a vast deal that was hitherto incomprehensible: the reason for those hours of despondency; for that bitterness toward people that we were quite conscious of, but never knew the cause of before; for that spiritual lassitude; yes, for the victory of that temptation that we hated and fought, yet could not overcome.

We see it all now. We are like a man who discovers a thief in his house — a discovery that explains many losses that he could not understand before. We have found that unbeknown to us, an enemy has entered the soul, taken up his abode there, and used its God-given powers to injure the soul and to dishonor God.

Such moments of insight reveal to us in a startling way how little we really know about our own inner life — how we have grown and developed and formed unconsciously to ourselves.

⚭

We are surprised at who we really are

But it is not only at such times as the first awakening that the soul is conscious of its ignorance of itself. As we advance in the spiritual life and in the practice of systematic self-examination, we are often surprised by the discovery of vast unknown tracts of the inner life of the soul. They seem like great plains stretching out in mystery and wrapped in mists that sometimes for a moment lift or sweep off and leave us looking for one brief instant upon great reaches of our own life, unknown, unmeasured, and unexplored. Men stand at such moments breathless in wonder and in awe, gazing upon these great tracts upon which they have never looked before, with kindling eyes and beating hearts; and while they look, the mists steal back until all is lost to sight once more, and they are left wondering whether what they saw was reality or the creation of their fancy.

Or sometimes they see, not far-stretching plains that fill the soul with an awestruck sense of its expansiveness and of how much has been left absolutely uncultivated, but mountain peaks climbing and reaching upward until lost in the heavens. Those peaks echo with the voice of many streams whose waters fertilize and enrich the small tracts of the soul's life that have been reclaimed and cultivated and that many a man has thought to be his whole inner self, even though he never asked himself where those rich streams had their source. Now he sees how their source lay in unmeasured heights of his own inner being whose existence he never dreamed of before. In one brief instant they have unveiled themselves.

He looks again, and they are shut out from his eyes; there is no visible token that he possesses such reaches, such heights of life. The commonplaces of his existence gather in and crowd upon him. The ordinary routine of life settles down upon him, limiting and confining him on all sides. The same unbroken line measures his horizon, such as he has always known it. The same round of interests and occupations crowd in upon his hours and fill them. The pressure of the hard facts of life upon him are as unmistakable and as leveling as ever, bidding him forget his dreams and meet and obey the requirements of the world in which he lives.

Yet the man who has caught but a momentary glimpse of that vast unknown inner life can never be the same as he was before. He must be better or worse, trying to explore and possess and cultivate that unknown world within him, or trying — oh, would that he could succeed! — to forget it. He has seen that alongside, or far out beyond the reach of, the commonplace life of routine, another life stretches away, he knows not where. He feels that he has greater capacities for good or evil than he ever imagined. He has, in a word, awakened with tremulous awe to the discovery that his life, which he has hitherto believed limited and confined to what he knew, reaches infinitely beyond his knowledge and is far greater than he ever dreamed.

∞

Sin and sanctity reveal us to ourselves

Such glimpses come to men at the most unexpected times and in ways it is impossible to account for, often in moments and under circumstances that we would have said were most unsuitable. I think it has probably been the experience of not a few to be startled almost in the act of some great sin, or before the excitement of it has well passed away, by a sudden reaction and a vivid breaking in upon their souls of the sense of great spiritual possibilities. The spiritual side has awakened to protest and convince the man that he is not wholly animal. Certainly there is no influence more deadly to the spiritual nature than sensuality, yet I venture to assert that in the moment after some grievous fall, many a man has been conscious of the deepest spiritual yearnings.

Such desires are not to be lightly put down to self-deception. They are in truth more real than the sensual; they rise up to face a man on the road to ruin and to show him clearer visions of the possibilities he is setting at naught.

Often such outbursts of spiritual longing, while yet the stain of sin lies deep and fresh upon the soul, lead men to do and say things that seem so unreal that those who know them well are tempted to call them hypocrites. But there is nothing further from their minds than hypocrisy; they are simply passing through one of those strange awakenings of the soul, in which they are torn with such convulsive movements in this direction and in that, toward the beasts and toward God, that in one instant they pass from the most degrading to the most spiritual frame of mind.

No wonder onlookers misjudge such men. They do not understand themselves. The sin has been the occasion of the momentary lifting of the mists that hung over the vast unknown heights of the inner life, and the man has been staggered by what he has seen.

Or again, how common it is for someone who lives a very self-indulgent, idle, easygoing life, who has never known what it is to forgo a pleasure, to come suddenly face-to-face with a person whose life is one constant act of sacrifice. Such a life appeals to certain sentiments that are dormant — if they are not developed — in every human heart. Here is seen the objective expression of those inarticulate feelings, and the soul is stirred to the depths. Buried beneath the oppressive and deadening influence of years of self-indulgence, the spirit of unselfishness and sacrifice is appealed to, and for one moment it rises and cries out, "Here I am! I, too, could once have led such a life as that." An unknown life, within the hardened crust that seemed to be the whole life, makes itself felt. The soul awakens to perceive possible heights and depths within it that it had never imagined.

On the other hand, what a strange scene and what a striking instance of men's ignorance of themselves was that at our Lord's Last Supper, when He said to the Apostles, "One of you shall betray me," and they began, every one of them, to say,

"Lord, is it I?"[4] No sooner had they been told that one of them would be guilty of this awful crime than the words seemed to act upon the Apostles with the strange result of revealing to each of them its possibility as they looked within. It seemed to them as if they were capable of unknown depths of evil, as doubtless under the stimulating presence of our Lord they daily had perceived new and yet unmeasured heights of devotion and sacrifice. The effect of our Lord's words on those holy men, amid all the sacred surroundings in which they were uttered, is a startling and typical instance of the way in which the sudden presentation to the mind of some great sin reveals to it possibilities of evil hitherto unthought of. The depths seem to open beneath and reveal unfathomed capacities of sin. Surely it is no exaggeration. The soul is capable of eternal growth in love and hate, and at such times, when any fresh knowledge of its capabilities is granted, even though it can see at most but a little way, it can feel the depths and the heights that are possible.

Such occasions as we have been considering give to the soul, in a moment, an outburst of light upon its inner self, revealing a vast, wide-reaching side of the character it never knew before.

∞

Changing circumstances show that
we do not know ourselves
But there are times — in some sense more bewildering — when a man is made aware not merely of what he was ignorant

---

[4] Matt. 26:21-22.

of in himself, but how completely he misunderstood himself, how different he really is from what he had thought himself to be. And I do not know whether there is any occasion that brings this out more strikingly, even alarmingly, than the effect of a sudden great change in the circumstances of his life.

What revelations have been disclosed by illness or by bodily or mental suffering? Under their rough handling, sometimes in a few years a character becomes so changed that it is almost impossible to recognize it. Yet we cannot say that suffering or sorrow made these changes, in the sense that they engendered in the soul characteristics that were not there before. No, they only developed them or revealed them. All unknown to that pleasant easygoing nature, there lay within it seeds — perhaps more than seeds — of discontent, bitterness, repining, and lavish selfishness. When the sun of prosperity sank behind the dark night of suffering, all this brood of evil awakened into active life.

How often, again, a person looks forward to some great event that will change the whole environment and interest of his life. A person anticipating such an event looks forward and plans and considers. He asks himself what effect this will produce upon his character: Will he be better or worse for it? Will it make him stronger or weaker? Will it draw out the spirit of sympathy or of antagonism? He imagines himself — and he has, perhaps, a very vivid imagination — in his new surroundings; he lives in them and brings all possible contingencies to bear upon himself that he may as much as possible gauge and measure himself so that he may not be taken unawares. At last the event so long anticipated comes to pass, and all the forecasts prove to be utterly wrong. The effect upon him is different altogether either from what he hoped it might be or feared it would be.

The man placed in the setting of circumstances different from those which he had long been used to finds that he is utterly unlike what he had imagined himself to be. His hopes and fears were alike miscalculations. He had planned that the same man as had known himself to be should be in these new surroundings. There was to him, as he looked forward to the change, only one uncertain quantity, and that was the new material or moral or religious world in which he was to find himself. As to these, he had made no mistake; the mistake lay in supposing that he knew the person who was to be placed amid these circumstances. There he was completely mistaken.

No sooner did the change take place than he found that he no longer knew the man. He was amazed to find himself wholly different from what he had imagined himself to be. New faults came to light; new virtues sprang to his defense; old temptations came to life in the new soil, and he found that the mere change of external things shows him to be altogether a different person from what he had thought.

It is one of the strange powers in human nature to weave so closely into the texture of its life things that are altogether external to it, that soon it fails to separate the personal source of thought and activity from the sphere of its actions. We get quickly into a mechanical round of life. We meet with the same people; we go through the same routine of duties; and the interaction of these external things day after day and year after year produces effects that we can readily see, but in the course of time, the outward things are lost sight of as causes, and we judge ourselves and our surroundings as one.

Someone has not, for instance, realized that the constant companionship of one who is full of gentleness and love draws out on his part a response of affection and gentleness that is not developed at all in other departments of his life or in dealing with other people. Yet because the surroundings of home are mellowed by influences that draw out a sympathetic response, the man looks upon himself and is considered by others as gentle and kind-hearted. He has never had his home disturbed by things that irritate him. The external things have so far responded to the interior tastes that, in this respect at any rate, he is wholly ignorant of what the effect of a constant jar between these would be. At last, in the course of years, the perfect adjustment between the outward surroundings and the inner state is so complete that the fact of their making, so to speak, but a mechanical combination is lost sight of, and the man looks upon himself and his environment as one and the selfsame thing. He has swung so long with the movements of the machinery that he has been unable to detect where the movement of the machinery ends and that of his own personality begins.

Then suddenly this combination comes to an end. He finds himself amid surroundings different from those he had been accustomed to, and these new circumstances act upon different elements in his character that had not in the former state of things been brought prominently forward. The result is that the man does not recognize himself; the effect of the change baffles all his forecasts, all his resolutions. He is at loose ends: external causes that used to produce quick response from within have ceased to act, and the response has consequently ceased to come; other things that acted as barriers to protect some weakness or defect from revealing or developing itself have been removed, and the effect of all this is much like that of removing the metal from the mold before the cooling process is completed.

Thus it happens that some great change that takes place in middle life acts as a revelation of character to many a person, revealing dispositions, defects, and habits of which they were wholly unconscious.

∞

Partial self-knowledge blinds us

Again, I think that not unfrequently the very knowledge that many possess of their own character blinds them to any deeper knowledge. There are in most people one or two more or less strongly marked characteristics — and, of course, multitudes of others no less real, although not so clearly defined. Now, it often happens that the mind is so constantly taken up with the observance of these more marked characteristics that these very subjects of interest and study keep it from going deeper and analyzing the more subtle and delicate movements that are taking place and having their way in the soul.

Indeed, this is sometimes the case to so great a degree that, while the mind is watching and taking pleasure in the action — and, as it may seem, development — of some well-defined virtue, it is utterly unconscious of the quiet working of a brood of petty vices and snarling passions that are steadily eating away the foundations of the very virtue upon which the attention is fixed. There have been moments when, if the people who fell prey to this had not been so blind, they might have felt the very edifice that they took for granted to be so strong shake and tremble beneath the assault of some temptation that had nothing directly to do with it. The foundations had begun to give way. Hidden away, so to speak, underground, out of sight, that hissing brood was at work, and he whose soul was the scene of all this remained in complete unconsciousness of what was in progress within him.

At last the work is completed, the virtue is undermined and falls. And then not uncommonly a curious thing takes place in the soul. The virtue that was almost a natural characteristic has filled so much space in the thoughts and life of the soul that the mind instinctively turns to look at the old landmark, and in a short time this virtue simply transplants itself from the moral life to the imagination. The person who practiced it for so long now begins to dream about it, and eventually to imagine that he practices it.

And this hideous and yet by no means uncommon trick that he has played upon himself is the outcome of being content to rest with a very partial and self-evident piece of self-knowledge. Had the person whose soul was the scene of this tragedy from the first formed the habit of sounding the unknown depths, of looking into those parts of his character that were hidden from him, such a disaster never could have happened.

The partial knowledge, therefore, that satisfies so many is in itself a very serious danger. In some cases, the mind will dwell, as we have been considering, upon some virtue that conceals from it a steady deterioration in other directions. When the conscience is for a moment awakened by a sense of uneasiness and a feeling that there is danger, it is lulled to rest by a few minutes' contemplation of the solid proportions of the virtue that fills the forefront of the soul. We are apt to think, for instance, when alarmed — it may be by the sense of powerlessness to pray and the consciousness of a growing separation from God — "After all, I can't be really falling away while I am so unselfish or so patient." This is the *pièce de résistance*; this it is to which the mind instinctively turns in moments of uncertainty; and this in fact so fills the horizon of the moral life that the eyes are blinded to the true condition of affairs.

In other cases, it is not virtue but a sin that blinds the soul to further knowledge of its true state. One grave sin, probably springing from the natural temperament, so absorbs the mind that it becomes incapable of perceiving a steady rallying of the powers and a stir and movement upward throughout the whole region of the moral life, which ought to fill it with hope, as the presage of a coming victory. Or, on the other hand, it may not see an ever-spreading deterioration, a springing up all over the inner life of the rank weeds of neglect.

The mind turns always to the same point, gauges all by that one sin. "*It* is no worse than it was; therefore, *I* am no worse," or "*It* is no better; therefore, *I* am no better." But it does not perceive how, although the sin itself seems stationary, the will is gradually weakening in all directions and losing all power to hold out against the pressure of any strong inclination, or, on the other hand, gradually growing in strength and purpose. The knowledge of that one sin closes the eyes to any further knowledge, even that of the baneful and deadly influence that is spreading from it throughout every department of the moral life.

There is a certain appearance of self-knowledge arising from the fact that, as the victim of this condition of things says, he knows how bad he is, whereas there is nothing further from the truth. He is unable to tell how bad he is except in this one particular, and in all else he knows neither how bad nor how good he is, or whether he is deteriorating or improving.

If, therefore, there is to be any spiritual growth, there must be a growth in self-knowledge. We cannot make any serious attempt to conquer our sins until we know what they are.

∞

Self-knowledge is greater than self-analysis

First, then, we must get our minds clear on one point that is likely to be very misleading. Self-knowledge, in the sense in which we use the word in the Christian life, is not by any means a necessary consequence of self-analysis. We may have a considerable power of self-analysis and display much skill in the way in which we are able to dissect ourselves, and yet have no proportionate self-knowledge. Self-analysis leads no more necessarily to self-knowledge than the analysis of another person's character necessarily involves the knowledge of that person. We know that it is not so with others; if we have any doubt about it, we can soon put it to the test.

Here is some public character who lives more or less before the world. You have watched and studied him closely, read all his utterances and tried in every way to get at the man's inner character. You have formed your estimate of it carefully and reasonably, and you say you know him through and through. Some time afterward, you meet this man, and somehow or other the first half-hour's interview leads you to alter all your conclusions. You see clearly that your analysis, so far as it went, was correct, but there were other things — it is impossible to say what — that you had not considered or that you knew nothing about: a tone, an atmosphere, that breathed around and through all that you had analyzed, giving its tone and color to all, and in a most unaccountable way modifying, if not wholly altering, your conclusions.

That something — that tone or color or whatever you may call it — is *personality;* it is that which combines and blends and harmonizes all the different parts of the character, bringing into working relations the most paradoxical elements. There is as much difference between the estimate you formed of the man by your analysis and that which has been the result of that half-hour's interview as there is between a thing that is dead and one that is living.

You smile as you think of the judgment you had formed of him before you met him. It was so true and yet so utterly false, so limited, so biased, so inharmonious. It was like a caricature. Yet, as you compare it with the true estimate you have now made, it is difficult to say where you went wrong, and still more difficult to discover how a few minutes' conversation has so altered your opinion.

It was not, by any means, merely owing to what he said, although now and again some few words seemed to send a shaft of light from his very heart and reveal it. But it was not that alone; it was that and a hundred other things too. The whole person radiated out influences that interpreted him — a look, a trick of manner, an expression, a tone of voice, who can tell what? Everything blended and harmonized a number of different, sometimes directly opposite, traits and produced that extraordinary impression that can be produced by personality alone. You had studied the man, so to speak, apart from his personality, and it was like trying to understand a man's expression by the study of his skeleton.

Now, it is, to a certain extent, the same with the study of ourselves. Self-knowledge is a far deeper and more comprehensive thing than self-analysis; indeed, we might have a very deep self-knowledge with little power of self-analysis. There is that subtle thing, the *self*, that has to be dealt with, which eludes all analysis.

I may know various things about myself. I may to a certain extent understand the working of my own mind. I may watch with interest the conflicting elements struggling for mastery within me. I may be intensely introspective and spend long periods of time in analyzing and docketing the litter that a day's work leaves scattered about my soul. Yet I may have never come face-to-face with that inmost self which sets the machinery I have been studying in motion and which blends all the scattered fragments of knowledge about myself that I have been able to bring together.

I think that this kind of self-knowledge, like the knowledge we gain through contact with another person, is moral rather than intellectual. Doubtless the intellect has its work and office in both cases, but as surely as we will never attain any intimate personal knowledge of another by the intellect alone, so surely we will never attain the knowledge of ourselves by it alone. Much, therefore, of the self-examination that takes not uncommonly the form of an intellectual pursuit after certain dimly defined characteristics that ever seek to escape our scrutiny, or of a strenuous effort to disentangle motives and aims as closely interwoven as a chemical combination — much of such self-examination fails to give the results that the time and labor and earnestness expended upon it deserve. The inmost self wraps itself up, like the silkworm in its cocoon, with the outcome of its industry and activity, and through this process of search we are but unraveling the silk thread, not getting to know the living center from which it was spun.

How, then, are we to get beneath the surface — to reach to the self? How are our self-examinations to reach any deeper than self-analysis? It is easy to state the difficulty that all are conscious of, but how is it to be met?

I would suggest one or two lines of thought which, if followed out, will, I think, at any rate put us somewhat in the way of self-knowledge.

∞

Learn to examine yourself
in the light of Christ

I believe that there are few people who have not at one time or another in their lives been startled by the power of self-revelation that comes to them through other people. I do not mean the judgments of others passed upon them — at any rate, not the spoken judgments; not even the silent unspoken judgments that come from look or manner, which are often more severe than those that are uttered in the sternest language. I mean the flash of light that often pierces through a dense fog of self-deception or of misunderstanding of ourselves, merely from the presence of another. There are few of us, I think, who cannot say to someone, "You have been the light of my life"; "In thy light I have seen light"; "Your life has been the light of my soul."

Christian Self-Mastery

Surely it is so. You have come for a moment into the presence of one whose life is a silent but most eloquent rebuke of the inmost tone and temper of your own life; and as you stand within the radiance of such a presence, you feel at once what you ought to be, what you might be, and what you have failed to be. Had you been told what now you see, you would not have believed it — no, you would have protested with honest indignation that the criticism was most unfair. But standing there in the presence of one who reflects in a remarkable way those virtues in which you especially fail — your characteristic failures hidden as they are from your own eyes — you see and judge yourself. Such is the mysterious power of personal life. In *his* completeness you see your own incompleteness; in *his* success, your own failure. A person, in all the strange attractiveness of character, comes before you — the incarnation of forgotten ideals and of unrealized ambitions, smothered and stifled under a rubbish heap of worldliness, selfishness, and sloth — and the living image of what you may once have dreamed you might be pierces through all that overlies and weighs upon the soul and calls forth a faint reflection in its mirror. Seeing what you might have been, you see what you are.

For instance, there is one who is living a life of utter selfishness, never denying a fancy or a desire, and complaining about every little unpleasantness that comes, as such things must come, into the most sheltered life. Such a person is brought by chance into the presence of one whose life is a prolonged act of physical suffering combined with ceaseless work for others. No word of judgment is spoken, but one of those two leaves the presence of the other self-revealed and self-condemned. The shabby and earth-stained reality stands face-to-face with the ideal fought for and attained, and in the light of that presence, it sees light.

Now, such experiences, real and most searching as they are, are but hints, pointing us to a still more perfect method by which to attain self-knowledge.

The more perfect the life that crosses our path, the clearer and more penetrating the light that it all unconsciously sends flooding our souls. Is it not possible, then, to bring ourselves into the presence of one who is absolutely perfect? Surely we can. And all the light that other lives shed upon us are but faint glimmers compared with that which flows from the presence of Jesus Christ. "His life is the light of men."[5] "In His light shall we see light"[6] in all its fullness.

Our self-examination deteriorates often, I think, into an often unilluminating piece of self-analysis, because it is, so to speak, conducted in the dark. It should be done in the presence of One who realizes all our noblest, often our forgotten, ideals. Our self-examination is not an abstract thing; it should be the comparison of ourselves with the most perfect, and at the same time most stimulating, standard.

What a different thing it is to rise from our self-examination with the knowledge that our prayers are poor and cold and feeble, but that we cannot help it — which may be perfectly true — than to rise with the knowledge gained from the comparison of our prayers in their coldness with the prayer of our Lord in His agony,[7] or the cry "My God, my God, why hast

[5] Cf. John 1:4.
[6] Cf. Ps. 35:10 (RSV = Ps. 36:9).
[7] Cf. Matt. 26:39.

Thou forsaken me?"[8] In this latter case, we have learned how mild and complacent has been our acceptance of coldness in prayer, or, on the other hand, how it has led us to cry out in our effort, to smart with the sense of loss as we utter the cry of dereliction. One state is the knowledge of a fact that may leave us no better, perhaps more indifferent as we get used to recognizing it with complacency. The other is a spiritual experience; it leaves the soul better or worse for the knowledge.

Again, how different it is to rise from our self-examination with the technical piece of dry, unradiating knowledge of the fact that today we have given way six times to irritation, whereas yesterday we gave way only five times, than to rise with the knowledge that has come to our soul from the comparison of ourselves in the presence of the irritating circumstances of our life with the example of our Lord, say, when He was struck on the face by one of the high priest's servants, or when He was in the presence of a Pharisee or Sadducee who was striving only to trap Him in His talk. The knowledge gained in the one case is purely intellectual; in the other case, it is far more — it is again a spiritual experience. In the presence of our Lord's unruffled calm, of His unfailing love, we see *ourselves* and are self-condemned. We get a moment's glimpse of a nature all sore and bitter and on its defense against men who are not loved; of an inner life of irritation and disturbance, where self reigns and all things are judged by the standard of our own personal taste.

The light from the presence of our Lord is that of which Simeon spoke: "This Child is set . . . that, out of many hearts,

---

[8]   Matt. 27:46.

thoughts may be revealed,"[9] and of which the psalmist spoke when he said, "Wherewithal shall a young man cleanse his ways, even by ruling himself after Thy Word"[10] — that Word which took flesh to be our example.

Therefore, if we would attain to any true self-knowledge, let our self-examinations be conducted in the presence of our Lord, with an ever-deepening knowledge of His personal life. Such examinations, however poor and low the life that is revealed by them, will not be discouraging, but will be found to be at once humbling and stimulating. "He killeth and He maketh alive. . . . He bringeth low and He lifteth up."[11] In that wondrous presence, there can be no lurking remnant of pride, still less of hopelessness. The revelation quickens hope and stimulates action.

∞

Test your self-knowledge

But once more, the great method of gaining any knowledge from nature is by experiment. Students of nature do not sit at home and speculate; they go out and question her. In a very true sense, the same may be said of the moral life. We are put here on earth, so to speak, to be questioned. And the answer that God listens for is not the answer of the lips but of action.

This is the true meaning of temptation. Each temptation is a question put to the soul. "What kind of a being are you? Do you love God or the following of your own inclinations?" Now,

[9] Luke 2:34-35.
[10] Cf. Ps. 118:9 (RSV = Ps. 119:9).
[11] Cf. 1 Kings 2:6-7. (RSV = 1 Sam. 2:6-7).

as God permits temptation as a means by which we reveal ourselves to be on His side or against Him, we cannot do better than resort to somewhat the same method to gain self-knowledge.

If you would attain to any real self-knowledge, therefore, do not be content with speculation as to what you may be, or what under certain circumstances you might be. *Test* yourself. Find out what you are by experiment. Do as you would do if you wished to gain any fresh knowledge of nature: question yourself by action.

For instance, you have a general and indefinite belief that you are not uncharitable or sharp-tongued or disposed to gossip. In your self-examination, you do not find any sharp rebuke of conscience in such matters. But do not be content with that. Put yourself time after time through the day to the test of experiment, and watch for the answer given you by facts. Resolve, for instance, in the morning to mortify yourself in speech so many times — half a dozen or a dozen times in the day. I think the result of a few days' efforts to keep such a resolution will be no small surprise to you of how much you fail, and how unfortified you are with your tongue.

There is nothing easier than to place ourselves in ideal states of mind; there is no ruder awakening than the facts that result from experiment. The first question put to nature in the form of experiment has exploded many a philosopher's dream, and one day's experiment in certain unexplored regions of the moral life has resulted in a rude but healthy awakening from mistaken dreams about himself.

Or again, you say and believe that you are not really self-indulgent, that you take your food and sleep for the sake of health, not for the pleasure they afford in themselves. Well, try this theory about yourself; test it by experiment. Resolve to practice a certain number of acts of mortification in the matters of food that in no way affect the health but merely the palate, or arrange for yourself the full measure of time that your health requires for sleep, and then rise promptly. Put these things to a few days' test, and see whether your theory about your indifference in matters of self-indulgence is correct.

The answers that such experiments give bring the conviction of truth and are often like rifts in the clouds that befog us, enabling us to get a true estimate of our strength and weakness. In the light of such experiences, self-examination becomes more serious and more real; we find after a few months that its character has changed in an unaccountable way, and that the best way in which the change can be described is by saying that the sphere of self-examination seems to be transferred from the study of details to the knowledge of a person. We are, no doubt, examining the details of daily life, but they are not mere isolated or dry facts: we see them emanating from a living person, whom we appear almost to have discovered, and it is the facts seen in the light of this personal life that change their whole character.

To use a comparison that is applicable within certain limits, it is like one watching the action and movements of bodies under the power of gravity before that law was discovered. Such a person would see a multitude of different acts, isolated and disconnected, moved in a manner that seemed more or less orderly, but without meaning and without connection. Then we may imagine the great discoverer, in the moment of his discovery, looking with kindling eyes and beating heart upon the same phenomena. Wherever he looks, all things are under the same law. An apple falling from a tree is like a beam of light through a sphere everywhere cracking and rent with fissures and showing the whole interior in a blaze of light. Before, he saw effects; now he sees effects in the light of their cause.

So it is with ourselves. The surface of our life gets somehow broken through, and we see the throbbing pulsation of that mysterious source of action: the self.

Chapter Two

∞

Discipline yourself

Whatever we may be able to learn from the study of nature, whether of art or science, all that we know of good and evil and of the great moral struggle, we know, apart from revelation, through our own nature alone. So imbued are our minds with moral ideas that we seem to see them reflected in the world of nature, but what we really see is only that extraordinary responsiveness with which she always meets man.

It is a strange thing, when we come to analyze it, that so much light and shade, so many lines and curves, so much inanimate matter should be able in such an extraordinary way to reflect the mind of man, that we even transfer to it our own moral ideas and struggles. Who has not felt that the skies and the earth and the winds not only can rejoice with us in our joys and sorrow with our sorrows, but that they echo our stormy passions, and reflect our wrath and rebellion and cruelty, and melt with us into tears of penitence and sing with us our *Te Deums*?

And yet all that we know of the moral life we know through our own nature alone. All else is but the reflection of what passes in the soul of man, the central and ruling figure upon earth.

We know of sin only as human sin, and we know of goodness and virtue only as seen through our own nature. When we think of the goodness and love of God, we think of these attributes as seen in and shown through the sacred humanity of Jesus Christ. When we think of diabolical wickedness, it is only human wickedness enlarged and intensified that we can imagine. Man stands midway between the seen and unseen, acted upon by the powers of good and evil, influenced and swayed by them, and the sensitive instrument through which they are revealed.

But here upon this earth, no knowledge of any moral kind, apart from that of revelation, can come to us except through our own nature. If it is to come here to man, it must enter through man's nature; it can come through no other door. It is only as uttered and expressed in terms of human nature that human beings can understand it. There may be forms of wickedness that evil spirits commit which human nature is incapable of and consequently knows nothing about. If man cannot commit these sins, how are they to become known here among men?

I know the human struggle, the human failure and victory. I can enter without difficulty into sympathy with the man whose temptations are very different from my own. Any evil or any good that has ever been done or is capable of being done by man, I can understand — its highest reaches, its lowest depths. I am moved to self-condemnation and to effort by the deeds of men infinitely above me, and I can feel the horrible fascination of the wickedness of men far worse than I. But with human nature my knowledge ends. The whole moral world is to me the world of men. As I look within, I know indeed full well that I stand among powers and beings that are not human; but I know them only as they act upon my heart and my mind and interpret themselves in terms of my own nature.

And who can doubt that this nature of ours is as capable of revealing evil as good? Indeed there are those who assure us that we know more about evil than about good. Certainly the great heights of the spiritual life are known to but a few, but I think that the utmost depths of wickedness are known perhaps to fewer.

At any rate, we cannot deny that alongside the wonderful revelations of goodness and virtue that have been made known through men and women, there has always been the dark shadow of sin. Our nature has shown us what sin is and has manifested a hideous power of adapting itself as the instrument of evil. It can reveal to us the perfection of virtue or of vice, as it seems, with equal facility.

I can think of people through whom I have seen shine the virtue of spotless purity, of perfect self-sacrifice, of unclouded sincerity and truthfulness, and I have seen in them the radiant beauty of which our nature is capable. But I know people also who have shown me to what depths of degradation human nature can sink.

If, then, man's nature is equally capable of good and evil, if the same human nature that shines with holiness in our Lord can become the prey of every evil desire and be possessed by a legion of evil spirits; if it can take delight in all that is holy and pure and of good report and be transported by the love of God and kindled with the desire for all that is noblest and best, and if it is equally capable of turning away from God and reveling in all that is worst and basest; if it is capable of being indwelt by the Holy Spirit or of being possessed by the Devil, the question arises: What is this evil that men commit so easily?

Is there in our nature some evil thing whose fermentations produce evil desires and evil actions? Could we, if we took man to pieces, find within him that which is the source of evil? If men are to become holy, are they to be instructed to destroy something in themselves that, having been destroyed, will enable them to become good?

Or, if this seems too material a view of evil, are there in man certain powers or forces that make for evil and certain others that make for good?

And shall we say that a bad man is one who has developed the forces of evil within himself, and a good man is one who has destroyed all these and developed the forces and powers that make for good? Does a man feel as he grows in holiness that he has gradually killed off certain powers that were apparently an integral part of himself, and that he has developed certain others? Does he feel as if the inner conflict has been one in which one part of himself was arrayed against the other, and that the victory of good over evil has been the victory of the higher powers by the killing off of the lower, and that consequently the triumph of good over evil has been purchased by a certain loss, as the victory of one army over another is won by the death of many a soldier?

It has seemed to some as if it were so. There are those who will tell you that there is a certain tameness about good people, a lack of fire and force and energy which is to be found in men who are not good; that the strongest men are not the men who are overly careful about the subdual of pride and temper and ambition and passion. They insist that such virtues, for instance, as are taught in the Beatitudes[12] and are essentially Christian — poverty of spirit, mourning, meekness — are lacking in virility and that there is an element of weakness in the ideal Christian character as compared with that of the man of the world. And it would be said, no doubt, that the reason for this is that the victory over evil and the triumph of these virtues is purchased at too great a price: the destruction of certain powers and of certain elements of our nature that we characterize as evil. The strong man needs to develop and to use everything with which he finds himself equipped, and to use all his powers is simply to be human.

∞

None of your human faculties are bad

Now, such a view of evil, as something positive, the fermentation of some evil substance or the possession of powers in themselves bad, is essentially unchristian. There is nothing — no substance, no power, no faculty — in man that is in itself bad. The Catholic doctrine of the Incarnation teaches that our Lord assumed our nature in its entirety and that whatever belongs to our nature was in Him. We cannot imagine that He assumed into union with His own divine personality anything that was inherently evil, or that, in creating man, He, the Creator, created and placed in him what was evil.

Analyze the soul of the greatest sinner and the greatest saint, and you will not find in the sinner any single element that is not in the saint. Compare the soul of the Magdalene or

---

[12] Matt. 5:3-12.

of St. Augustine[13] before and after their conversion. There was nothing lacking in either after their conversion that was there before. As saints they were not weakened or emasculated. Who, on reading their history, does not feel that their lives after their conversion were the lives of those who had "come to themselves," that they were then their real selves, that somehow they got the power of self-expression in the fullest and highest sense? They lost nothing, destroyed nothing, but were in full possession of all their powers.

There was much in the Magdalene that she had never used, perhaps never dreamed of, until she came to our Lord. He revealed to her the secret of true self-development, which is another word for *sanctity*. And she found under His guidance that everything in her had henceforth to be used, and used in a fuller and richer way than she had ever imagined possible. It was in no narrow school of self-limitation, in no morbid school of false asceticism, that this poor sinner was educated in the principles of sanctity, but in the large and merciful school of Him who has been ever since the hope of the hopeless, the friend of publicans and sinners; who knows full well that what men need is not to crush and kill their powers, but to find their true use and to use them; that holiness is not the emptying of life, but the filling; that despair has wrapped its dark cloud around many a soul because it found itself in possession of powers that it abused and could not destroy and did not know how to use. Christ taught them the great and inspiring doctrine "I am not come to destroy, but to fulfill."[14]

---

[13] St. Augustine (354-430), Bishop of Hippo.
[14] Matt. 5:17.

If there is a lack of strength or virility in good people, it is not because they are good, but because their goodness is imperfect, or of a spurious kind. In proportion as a man is really good, he will be strong. We often forget that the Apostle of Love, who is so frequently represented in art as almost effeminate, was in fact "the Son of Thunder."[15] The gentlest of the saints will be found to be really stronger than many a one who is not a saint but has gained a character for strength. Holy people often surprise us by showing a courage and firmness for which we did not give them credit. The weakness with which they are credited arises from their view of life: they do not care to make a stand or to fight for many things that ordinary people set a high value upon, because they do not think them worth it.

For the difference between goodness and badness does not consist in the presence or absence, the preservation or destruction, of anything within us that is evil, but in the right or wrong use of powers in themselves good. Sin is the misuse of powers that God has given us, the use of them for ends for which they were never intended. It is like a soldier taking the sword he was given to defend his country and using it in the cause of her enemies.

Every power, every faculty, every gift of our nature was given to us for good. They were given us for the service of God and are capable of being used in His service. When we take these God-given powers and use them for an unworthy end, we sin. The heart with which I can rise up into the closest union with God I can use in loving what God most hates. The heart of the greatest sinner is the same faculty and is capable of

---

[15] Cf. Mark 3:17.

the same acts as the heart of the greatest saint. It is not the heart itself that is evil. The most degraded and vicious of men have the same divine power of love as the holiest. The difference is that one has set his affections on an object unworthy of them, and the other has turned to Him who has made our hearts for Himself.

So, again, it is the same will with which I choose right that I can use in choosing wrong. The will is good whatever I use it for. In choosing evil, I violate my whole nature and weaken my will. In choosing good, I act according to my nature, and my will grows stronger and ever more reliable.

The will that has been most enslaved by the constant choice of all that is base and vile, and which seems incapable of making one good choice — even such a will is in itself good. The evil lies not in the will but in the objects upon which it exercises its choice. The evil is the abuse of a great and noble power. To become good, you have not to destroy it or rid it of anything inherent in it, still less to lay it aside unused, but rather to use it, weakened and debased as it is, in the energetic choice of good.

Thus we might take one after another of those powers that have been the cause of the greatest sin, and see how, although the instruments of sin, they are in themselves good and in the use of them, the saints became saints.

Augustine did not lay aside his great intellectual gifts when he gave up his Manichaean errors and became the servant of Christ. We see, rather, the emancipation of his intellect. The Truth made him free.[16] Augustine's intellect apparently got a

---

[16] Cf. John 8:32.

new expansion when he turned it to the Truth. It was as though a great power that had been cramped and distorted and was never able to use itself to the full was at last set free to exercise itself upon objects worthy of it.

∞

Turn your God-given powers to the good

It is necessary to be quite clear on this point, for upon it will depend our whole view of the reformation of life and character. If you are struggling to destroy the evil that you believe to be in you, it is indeed a hopeless task, and you are condemned to failure at the start. If, on the other hand, you realize that the change from a life of sin to a life of holiness is but a change in the objects upon which you exercise the powers God has given you, you will feel that it is by no means hopeless — on the contrary, that it is pre-eminently reasonable.

There is infinite inspiration in the thought that you are striving to use your powers for the very purpose for which they were created. If you know that your heart was created to love God, there may be great difficulties in training it to turn away from unworthy objects, but you cannot doubt that it *can* love God. Only strive long enough, therefore, and you must succeed.

There are not a few, I think, who, if they could realize this, would feel that it is just what they need to give a stimulus and inspiration to their whole life. To them, mortification means death, not life. They are striving to kill what will not be killed. In their hearts they feel that the spiritual life is rather an empty life; many things that they used to do they feel that they must not do, but they find nothing else to fill the place of what they have given up. Their reason tells them that mere repression is not life. Yet in the past, they found so much sin mixed up with most of what they did that the only alternative seems *not* to do, and one thing after another has been given up.

Study yourself, examine the structure of your being, and one thing will impress you: every faculty of your mind, every power, every member of your body was made for action. The body is the instrument of the mind's action; the senses are the channels through which it is fed. The eye was made to look, to see, to gaze upon things outside.

If, in penitence for sins they have committed, a man closes his eyes and will not look upon the fair scenes and sights of God's creation, he should know that this is only temporary and as an act of penitence and discipline, so that he may gain control and bring them from wandering and wantonness to use them better and with true freedom in the service of the soul. The servant has assumed too much independence — rather, has begun to rule his master, and he must be taught his place. So with everything.

The hand was made for action, the mind to think, the will to choose, and the heart to love. The tongue was made for speech, not silence. If it has been used for evil, it must be trained and disciplined so that it may be used for good. Many a time, indeed, when it fain would speak, it has to be forced to keep silence. Why? Not merely so that it may simply become an idle and useless member of the household of the soul, but so that it may become what it was intended to be: the instrument of the soul's utterance in the service of God.

Mortification, therefore, is not an end in itself; it is but a means to an end, and the end is the truest and fullest use of everything we have. " 'Tis life, not death, for which we pant": the death is a death unto sin as the means of entering into a larger life unto righteousness. Self-discipline must necessarily be in proportion to the misuse of any sense or power, but it is the true use of it that we aim at in every act of self-discipline.

"For the joy that is set before us we endure the cross":[17] we do not endure it merely for its own sake, but for what lies beyond it. And we bear those acts of self-denial and self-restraint because we feel and know full well that through such acts alone can we regain the mastery over all our misused powers and learn to use them with a vigor and a joy such as we have never known before.

There is nothing morbid in such acts of restraint of mortification. They are full of promise. They are full of hope. There are times when, chafing perhaps under the restraint that is put upon them, for a moment our powers find their true outlet and break away with bounding joy in the channels prepared for them. Such moments are a pledge of what is to come, and they strengthen us in our hard task.

The lips that were often sealed in penitential silence for bitter words, for unkind criticism, irreverence, or unrestrained chatter, find moments when they can make amends and heal by loving words those they have wounded in the past, or speak with the burning eloquence of strong conviction for the Faith they have once blasphemed. The hands that have done evil deeds and suffered under the discipline of restraint find moments when they are used in the service of kindness and charity and fill the heart with a joy that was worth waiting for. And

---

[17] Cf. Heb. 12:2.

then the penitent soul cries out, "I know now that all these gifts of God are good and were made for use, not merely for repression. I am bringing these wanderers back into the true way of life, these rebel servants to be my helpers in the service of God."

This, I think, is what St. Paul means when he says, "As you have yielded your members to serve uncleanness, and iniquity, unto iniquity; so now yield your members to serve justice, unto sanctification."[18] And again, "Let not sin therefore reign in your mortal body; . . . neither yield ye your members as instruments of iniquity unto sin, but present yourselves unto God, as those that are alive from the dead, and your members as instruments of justice unto God."[19]

The picture before his mind is a vivid one. He sees the soul as the servant of sin and using all its members, faculties, and senses in the service of sin, and increasing thus the sway of sin — eye, ear, hand, heart, and imagination working for sin, in its service, and dragging the soul down.

Well, St. Paul says, I do not ask you to give up the use of one of these powers, or to leave them idle: I ask you to give yourself no longer to sin, but to God, as one alive from the dead, and then use every power you have in the service of God as instruments of justice unto holiness. Use them for the very purpose for which they were given. It is in the splendid energy of positive action that the morbid power of sin is to be overthrown. Let God reign in your heart, and you will find plenty of work for head and hand.

[18] Rom. 6:19.
[19] Rom. 6:12-13.

Of course, between this vigorous living in the full and free exercise of all the powers and the life of sin, there lies that period of discipline and mortification in which the misused powers have to be restrained and checked and trained for their true work. A man who all his life used his imagination for evil will not find it easy to use it as the handmaid of faith. There will be revolts and relapses, and the pictures of the past from which he has turned he will find often vividly mirrored upon it. There will be days of darkness when it will seem to him as if he has undertaken an impossible task.

But he will be sustained by two thoughts: that this misused faculty, however defiled, however much disordered, is in itself good, and that only in using it for that for which it was given can it be redeemed. These thoughts will sustain him and encourage him to bear the suffering that is the price of its redemption.

It is as though one who had a great talent for music but had no technical training, and consequently could never produce the best results of his art, were to put himself under a great master. The first lessons he will have to learn will be, for the most part, to correct his mistakes, not to do this and not to do that. It will seem to him that he has lost all his former freedom of expression, that he is held back by all sorts of technical rules, that whenever he seeks to let himself go, he is checked and hampered. And it is no doubt true.

But he will soon begin to realize that as he learns more and suffers in the learning, possibilities of utterance reveal themselves that he has never dreamed of. He knows, he feels, that he is on the right path, and as the channels are prepared and the barriers against the old bad methods more firmly fixed, he feels the mighty tide of his genius rise and swell; he hears the shout of the gathering waters as they sweep before them every obstacle and pour forth in a mad torrent of glorious sound. All those days of restraint and suffering are crowned with the joy of the full and perfect expression of his art. The restraint and discipline he knew full well in those seemingly unfruitful days were but the means to an end. The end is always before him, and the end is positive expression. The dying to his old untrained and bad methods is but the birth throes of a larger and richer action — verily "for the joy that was set before him, he endured the cross" of discipline.

This is the true principle of all Christian self-discipline. Without such an inspiring motive, it is meaningless; it is cruel self-torture. We need — who does not know it? — to fill our life, not to empty it. Life is too strong a thing, our nature is too positive, to be content with mere restraint and repression. Many a soul who has given up one thing after another and emptied its life of interest after interest, learns to its dismay that its energies, finding no means of expression, turn inward and revenge themselves in morbid self-analysis and sickly scruples. They need an outlet; they need interests. You may check the flow of a stream while you are preparing to divert its channel, but you cannot stop it. If you try, it will only gather force behind the barriers that hold it back, beat them down, and rush through with a strength and volume all the greater for the restraint.

And the stream of life cannot be merely held back. Many a man trying thus to repress himself finds after a time that temptations have only grown stronger and passions more violent, and that he seems to have become worse rather than better through the temporary resistance. What he needed, what might have protected him from failure and despair, was to be taught that all the restraint was but temporary and in order to turn the stream into its true channel.

∞

Subdue your rebellious will

But again, we all know the tendency that there is in the different powers of our nature to assume an independent life, to live and act not for the good of the person, but simply for their own gratification, often to the great injury of the person. The central power, if it is not constantly on the watch, loses control, and the members of the body and the powers of the mind take matters into their own hands and live for themselves.

We are often scarcely conscious of this until we wake up to find that we have lost control of ourselves — that one after another of our senses and faculties (our "members," as St. Paul calls them) refuses to obey us and is living its own separate life; more than that, that they often make factions and combine to dethrone conscience and place some base passion, it may be, to rule its place. There is a well-organized revolution taking place, so quiet that conscience is scarcely alarmed until it finds its power is well-nigh gone.

Many a man living an easy, self-indulgent life is startled to find all unknown to him a deadly alliance between the senses and the imagination against reason and conscience, and that a civil war has already begun — that conscience has almost lost all power of command and the will is in chains. Or again, he finds that the heart, intent upon its own gratification, has called in imagination to its aid and seduced the reason itself from its natural alliance with conscience to help it to gain its own ends.

And each sense, each faculty, in proportion as it lives for itself, gathers strength as it absorbs into itself the life that was meant to feed the whole nature, and thus exhausts and enfeebles the rest. There are men whose intellects seem to have dried up and absorbed the life of the affections, and there are others in whom one passion has grown to such enormous proportions that there is life and nourishment left for little else.

This breaking up of the soul's unity and strength is the result very often, not of any conscious act on the part of the individual, but merely of neglect, of leaving his nature to take its own course and follow its own inclinations. "Eternal vigilance is the price of liberty,"[20] and we must exercise this vigilance unceasingly over every department of our being, every sense, every faculty, and every inclination, if we would keep ourselves free.

> One tyrannous single thought, one fit
> Of passion, can subdue the soul to it.

It is indeed a strange subversion of the order of nature that a man cannot use his powers with such uncontrolled freedom as he would like, but that they seem to use him; that he does not think of what he wishes, but that his mind seems to have broken away from his control and to have its own thoughts; that he does not love that which he knows is worthy of his

---

[20] Wendell Phillips, Speech before the Massachusetts Antislavery Society, 1852.

affections, but that his heart draws him to that which reason and conscience abhor.

Yet it is true. Who does not know what it is to find some part of his nature acting in direct defiance of his will? At first it seems as if the disobedience were not deliberate, as if it were a lack of sufficient care on our own part, and we need only to be a little more firm and peremptory in command. But soon there is left no possibility of doubt: the will issues the command, and it is defiantly disobeyed.

A person knows, for instance, that dwelling upon certain memories is bad for him, bad in every way, making him morbid, paralyzing his powers and rendering him incapable of doing his work. He determines that he will close the door of his memory against the return of these thoughts. He does not wish to recall them; he deliberately wishes and decides to forget them; and he issues his command to the memory to forget them. But he finds to his dismay that this faculty, which is but a part of himself and has no existence apart from him, seems somehow to have developed a life of its own, a life that apparently has passed out of his control and that seeks its own gratification, not his good, and simply ignores his command.

Where does it get this life? Where does it get this will of its own? How can it act except as a faculty of his mind, an integral part of himself? It is *his* memory, *his* power of looking backward, yet there it is, living and acting as if it had an individuality of its own, a source of evil to the person by whose life it lives. Well may he ask, "How can this be?" Yet who does not know that it is true?

Or perhaps it is not the memory but the heart. The heart has begun to love what reason and conscience forbid. The reason ridicules it, the conscience issues its stern commands, but the heart with a mighty sweep of passion carries all before it and, amid the protests of conscience and the dictates of reason, has its own way.

∞

Control your other powers and faculties

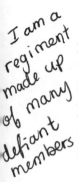

I am a regiment made up of many defiant members

Now, it is the office of self-discipline to bring all these rebel powers back under obedience, to allow no dual authority throughout the kingdom of the soul; to see that no part of the nature develops any life of its own, but that all cooperate for its well-being; that no sense or faculty acts or lives merely for its own gratification, but for the good of the person to whom it belongs.

This is the work of self-discipline that lies before every man who, through carelessness, self-indulgence, or sin, has lost in any degree the power of self-command. His faculties have gotten out of control and wandered after their own fancies. They must learn that they can be of service in the kingdom of the soul only as they obey the sovereign authority of the will and cooperate with all the other powers for its well-being. But he must let these undisciplined faculties know that they have their place and their work, and that when they have learned control, they will do better work and have a deeper satisfaction in it and a larger freedom than they ever had in the days of their wildest license.

The vagrant off the streets, who has never known what it was to check an impulse or obey a command, finds at first the discipline of the drill ground discouraging work, often well-nigh intolerable. But he sees what it has done for others. He is inspired with a belief that it will make a man of him, and he is soon conscious of the invigorating influence of solidarity, the thrill of the multitude, and the power that comes through co-operation and through surrender to authority.

Even so we must collect our vagrant powers and faculties and train them to the word of command and teach them to keep step, holding the more eager and impulsive back and urging the sluggish forward, dealing patiently with each raw recruit that has been won from a life of slackness and independence to join in the service of the great army of the *patria* of the soul.

more army imagery :)

The discipline and strictness of the drill ground will be felt by each — even the very lowliest member of the body or the humblest power of the soul — to be no unmeaning check to its action but a great and inspiring preparation for a better work than it ever did before, each cooperating with the rest, and all moving forward at the word of command of conscience, to do battle against the enemies of the soul. How different are such results from the isolated skirmishes, when friend was often mistaken for foe, and the days of riot and pillage when these vagrant powers fought or feasted as they pleased, having no clear aim before them, recognizing no authority and obeying no word of command.

We must discipline, therefore, all our powers of mind and body to cooperate for the well-being of the person. We must bring them back from their lax life of idleness or isolation and teach them that only by working with all the other powers of the soul can any of them do its best work. We must teach them that, as the general cannot fight without his soldiers, no more can the most brilliant faculty of the mind do its work perfectly without the humblest and poorest; that as "the eye cannot say unto the hand, I have no need of thee, nor the head to the feet, I have no need of you,"[21] no more can the head say to the heart, "I have no need of thee," nor the reason to the emotions, "I have no need of you." We must bring them back and train them so that they may work in obedience and that they may work together — teaching some to wait, forcing others to action, punishing some, and encouraging others. We must force any passion or any faculty that has pushed itself into a position of undue prominence or command to take for a time the lowest place, punishing it if it be necessary, often even reducing its strength and rebellious spirit by starvation, but only so that it may learn to do its work better.

Such discipline is no unreasonable restraint upon our powers. Its purpose is to restore to the soul the exercise of its full power, which lies in that order and cooperation upon which its unity depends. It requires three things:

• *Patience:* In the practice of self-discipline, we need patience. Impatience, too great an anxiety to see quick results of our efforts, will only delay the work. We are dealing with the most delicate instruments, which can very easily be put out of gear. We must not be discouraged if the neglect or abuse of years takes years to rectify. The mind is a very delicate instrument, and if it is overstrained, its elasticity will be destroyed. Many an act of self-discipline that we know is good we may not be able to practice except in the course of time.

Don't be too hard on yourself!

[21] Cf. 1 Cor. 12:21.

A very little overpressure may cause a reaction that will make the last state worse than the first. We must season the materials before we can bend them to our will. It is impossible to make sweeping reforms and sudden changes. Habits, whether good or bad, are formed only by constantly repeated acts; a very little done day by day and persevered in will effect more than can ever be effected by violence. It is good to remember that there is such a thing as undisciplined efforts at self-discipline. Needless to say, such efforts always end in failure. We have to treat the wayward faculty or the wanton sense as we would treat a spoiled child, to win it back little by little, and with unwearied patience, knowing well that any effort at compulsion will certainly end in revolt.

• *Prudence:* And we need prudence. It is always good to remember that we have no right to think that the goodness of a cause can ever exempt a person from the ordinary laws of prudence in the method of carrying it out; still less are we to expect that God will remedy the effects of our imprudence. The work of grace is always dependent upon a foundation built upon the laws of nature. If a person overstrains his mind by too much prayer, his mind will suffer just as much as if it were overstrained by too much study; the fact that the intention was good does not alter the result of a foolish action.

And so a man cannot easily forgo all that he has been habituated to by years of self-indulgence. Whatever is in itself wrong, of course, he can and must forgo,

steady not merely impassioned resolve

for wrongdoing is never useful or necessary. But in regard to giving up what is not wrong, he must hasten slowly. Prudence must ever stand by his side and speak her word of wisdom at every step of the way. The pampered body will rebel only if it is handled roughly. Under the guidance of prudence, it must be trained by degrees to do without those things that by long use have become almost necessary to it. We must return to a normal life before we can hope to be able to endure an ascetic life. And the mind that has been left so long in unrestrained license or in sluggish inaction must not be brought suddenly under restraint, but it must gradually and gently be won to accept the wise and patient discipline that it recognizes as its liberator from the slavery into which it has fallen.

• *Grace:* Finally, we need to look constantly for the assistance of divine grace. We cannot act alone in the work of restoration, nor can we be restored merely to a state of mended and repaired nature. The remedies that God supplies are supernatural, and if we are to be restored at all, we will have to rise higher than we could by nature. God pours into our wounds the oil and wine of divine grace, so that as the wounds are healed, the medicine that heals them transforms our nature and endows it with a new vigor.

The struggle to be merely natural, moral, masters of ourselves quickly teaches us that this is impossible. The work is beyond us. We cannot become merely what we were before; we must become more. If we wish to restrain ourselves and recover ourselves, we must call in the Great Physician, and in His hands we shall find a new life instilled into us and a new world open out before our kindling eyes.

Chapter Three

∞

Abide by the laws
of the spirit

∞

The spiritual life of most people may be said to begin from one of two starting points: the thought of God or the thought of self. There are many whose minds turn to God with a natural instinct. The things of faith have ever been a reality to them. Even when their lives have been most inconsistent, their faith has shone clear and undisturbed.

There are others who have been driven to God through the knowledge of their own great needs. The natural tendency of their minds is to turn inward, not outward. They have been driven to look outward and upward by what they have found within.

Their knowledge of themselves, of the strength of natural inclination, of their own temperament, and of the power and persistency of habit deepens their sense of hopelessness and shows them that they have no power of themselves to help themselves, and only when, like the woman in the Gospel, they have "suffered many things from many physicians . . . and were nothing the better, but rather worse,"[22] they are driven at last to God.

[22] Mark 5:26.

If there had anywhere appeared in space
Another place of refuge where to flee,
Our souls had sought for refuge in that place
And not in Thee. . . .

And only when we found in earth and air
And Heaven and Hell, that such could nowhere be,
That we could not flee from Thee anywhere,
We fled to Thee.[23]

Self-knowledge apart from God can indeed lead only to despair. For he who has sunk to earth knows well he can find no lever on earth or within himself to raise himself. How can he? How can anything within him raise him above himself? How can anything on earth raise him above the earth? Like the piece of silver in the parable, that has fallen to the earth, he needs the hand of Another to raise him.

From one or the other, therefore, of these two starting points, the religious life of most men will be found to begin: from the knowledge of God or the knowledge of self.

But although they may begin from either of these two poles — earth or Heaven — the end must be the same. From the greatness and holiness of God, one will learn the greatness of the destiny of man, to whom He has condescended to reveal Himself. The other, from the greatness of his own needs, will learn the greatness and the love of God, who delivers him. For, as it has been well said, "He who believes humanity requires no higher influence than its own will see in Christ no more than a man like himself; he who thinks man's only need is an example will look upon Christ as an ideal man; he who thinks man only needs virtue will look upon Him as a great moral teacher. But he who feels that the need of his na-ture is something more than nature can supply will seek for the supernatural in Christ."

Now, there are in the Apostolic College two men who sev-erally represent these two starting points of Christian knowl-edge and life: St. John and St. Paul.

St. John is the type of the objective mind. He looks upward and outward. Like the eagle, he spreads his wings and soars aloft and gazes into the face of the Sun. In all his writings he tells us little or nothing about himself. He lets us into none of the secrets of his own inner struggles. We know him mainly as the mirror in which the Person of Christ is reflected. He is the divine — the great contemplative. He is like that "sea of glass like unto crystal" of which he writes "that is before the throne of God."[24] When he speaks of himself at all, it is almost imper-sonally: he is "the disciple whom Jesus loved."[25] He is the disci-ple who leaned upon Jesus' bosom at the Last Supper, the one whose life was "hidden with Christ in God."[26]

What can we learn from him directly of the mysteries of the human soul, of the conflict with evil, of the anguish of peni-tence and the haunting memories of sin? He tells us indeed of the infinite love of God. He is the Apostle of Love, and he re-veals to us the greatness of the destiny of man, who can rise into such intimate and close friendship with the Most High.

[24] Cf. Rev. 4:6.
[25] John 21:7.
[26] Cf. John 21:20; Col. 3:3.

How different, on the other hand, is St. Paul. There is no secret of the human heart that he does not know. His experiences are for the world. He gives them all freely and generously to mankind. He has that wonderful and rare charm: the power of speaking of himself without a shadow of egotism. He tells us of his own idealism and of his utter powerlessness to realize his ideals, and how at last he gained the power. Whatever he tells us comes with the freshness and vividness of a personal experience.

St. John, if I may say so, stands behind his writings. St. Paul stands in the forefront. The personal element is everywhere. Across the ages, St. Paul lives before us; his words throb and vibrate with an intense personality rarely equaled and never surpassed. He is the representative of the subjective mind, looking inward, studying, analyzing, and recording its own workings.

We could ill afford to do without the revelation of both of these apostles. One will appeal more to one type of character, the other to another; but we need both. St. John is like the great arching heavens above us, calm in their serenity; St. Paul like the storm-swept world beneath. But as earth and heavens can never be separated, so these two great teachers together are needed to show us the way in which man can be united to God.

∞

Conquer your sins with more than self-knowledge

Now, it is certainly untrue to say that the one thing we need to overcome sin and to attain perfection is a more perfect knowledge of our own nature and its laws. We do not find that the best physiologists and the best psychologists are necessarily the best men. Indeed, if we know ourselves at all, we are painfully conscious that under great temptation, we often act in direct opposition to our knowledge. The drunkard and the sensualist know full well that they are ruining the health of both mind and body, but I doubt if this knowledge alone has ever succeeded in making one or the other either temperate or pure. Indeed, according to the teaching of our Lord, this is taken for granted: "He that knew his Lord's will and did it not, shall be beaten with many stripes."[27]

The mere knowledge of what we ought not to do, often even of the disastrous results of what we are tempted to, will not necessarily hold us back from doing it. St. Paul utters the experience of every man who has ever striven after a high standard when he says, "I cannot do the things that I would," and again, "The good which I will, I do not; but the evil which I will not, that I do."[28]

Yet at the same time, although it is certainly not the whole truth to say that ignorance is the only cause, or the chief cause, of failure, there is undoubtedly an element of truth in it. Many a life's failure has been caused by ignorance. Many an earnest person has lost all the joy and conscious success in the spiritual life through not understanding himself. If we understood ourselves better, we would certainly be able to put ourselves to better use.

There are not a few who have failed through striving for the impossible. A failure to obey the laws of our physical nature

[27] Cf. Luke 12:47.
[28] Cf. Rom. 7:18-19.

will cause ill health or death. The violation of the laws that govern the working of the mind may cause insanity, and the ignorance of these laws has made shipwreck of the spiritual life of not a few. And ignorance of the higher and more subtle and mysterious laws of our inmost being must cause failure and suffering in proportion.

The truth is, we need both to know ourselves and the laws that govern our lives, and also to know and to apply the remedies God has provided to heal the diseases caused by the violation of these laws.

Yet it is no doubt true that no two men are exactly alike either in their character or experience. Each individual to a certain extent must stand alone.

Most of us, I suppose, have felt that in the greatest moments of life, when some serious choice had to be made or some great temptation faced, we could get little help from others, except the kindly help that comes from the sympathy of a fellow creature. At such moments, everyone feels the isolation of his own personality. It is impossible to put into words so that another can understand just what makes the difficulty *my* difficulty.

But, on the other hand, so alike are the workings of the human heart in all, so really one is human nature, that the knowledge of ourselves helps us understand others, and it is possible so to analyze the structure and working of the soul as to be able to get some knowledge of the causes and results of those inner struggles that are the common lot of mankind. The temptations and disposition of one may be very different from those of another, yet the causes of temptation and of failure or success may be — assuredly are — the same in all.

To this knowledge St. Paul shall be our guide. As we study his wonderful analysis of himself and the inner conflict he experiences and describes, we feel as if he were reading the very secrets of our hearts; and more, we understand ourselves and the tortuous workings of our nature as we never did before. And, as in the case of all great masters, what he discloses is so simple, so natural, and so true that we almost wonder why we did not guess it ourselves.

∞

Conflict will always rend your soul
In the first place, he describes for us that inner struggle that goes on ceaselessly in every human heart. Man is not at one with himself. His soul is like a household divided against itself; often it is like a kingdom in a state of revolution. This inner conflict is not the conflict between the flesh and the spirit — the flesh lusting against the spirit and the spirit against the flesh.[29] It is far deeper and more intimate; it is within the very springs of our being.

The inner soul is not at one with itself. It has to decide and to act often — in some things, most often — in the teeth of a deadly opposition, and the opposition arises from no outside source, but from within. If the whole soul, the person at one with himself, had to meet opposition or temptation from without, it would be a comparatively easy matter, but he who goes forth to battle does not feel sure of his troops; he knows that half will oppose him and that, in the battle, he cannot be sure of having his resources at command. While fighting with some

[29] Cf. Gal. 5:17.

foe from without, he has at the same time to fight a more dangerous foe within, who at any moment may hand him over, bound and captive, to the enemy.

This is that inner conflict St. Paul describes with a master's hand in the seventh chapter of his letter to the Romans. We all know it; we all experience it daily, yet we scarcely realize how anomalous it is. There is nothing like it so far as we know upon earth. Every other living thing is at one with itself, although, it may be, at war with all the world.

We cannot imagine that the beast has to wage any inner conflict with itself in order that it may live according to the laws of its animal life. Whatever may be the struggle for life with its environment, every instinct, impulse, and passion cooperates for its well-being and to lead it to its end. The dim light that shines within is sufficient to enable it to see things only as they exist in relation to its narrow and circumscribed life. It is disturbed by no misleading appearances from without, by no false lights within. The whole machinery of its being cooperates to lead it directly to its end.

The tree spins its wondrous web, shaping branch and bud and blossom and fruit with unerring certainty and steady purpose. It never pauses, never makes a false start, and never tries another model. It knows only what it needs to perfect its own life. Amid a multitude of other lives different from it, it lives content. Its perfection results from its perfect unity; all its resources are at its command and cooperate for its well-being.

Man alone, amid all these living things around him, lord of them all and using them for his service, is not master of himself. He is torn and tortured by the inner struggle, the incapacity to rally all the forces within him to pursue his end and

attain to his own perfection. What success can he look for until this is secured? How can he meet some seductive temptation with any hope of victory when he knows already that his
heart desires and is determined to have what his reason tells
him will be his ruin?

∞

Your mind and your will are at odds

But again, St. Paul shows us the seat of this inner conflict.
It lies in the highest region of the soul's life. There is discord in
the council chamber of the soul, and the whole kingdom suffers from the lack of union among its rulers. The revolt or disobedience of the humblest servant or the lowest official in its
service springs from this. Every department feels it and suffers
from it.

The conflict is primarily between the moral and intellectual powers. The mind and will are not at one. The mind sees
and delights in what is good, and the will chooses what is evil.
"I am delighted," says St. Paul, "with the law of God according
to the inward man; but I see another law in my members,
fighting against the law of my mind, and captivating me in the
law of sin that is in my members."[30] The order of nature is overthrown; the will refuses to obey the guidance of reason. The
legislative and executive are in open conflict. What the mind
desires, the will refuses to carry out.

Who does not know this? Who has not experienced it: the
hatred of the sins we commit and continue to commit; the
love of the good we desire and intend to do, and yet often do

[30] Rom. 7:22-23.

not even try to do; the will going its own way in direct disobedience to the reason? We admire and wish for self-control and hate ourselves for the impulsiveness to which we yield. We love the spirit of unworldliness and are worldly to the heart's core. We hate insincerity and are eloquent in the praise of truth and are thoroughly untruthful.

And this opposition between our ideals and acts does not in any way arise from hypocrisy, but from the fact that "we cannot do the things that we would." Here in the highest region of the soul's life there is discord. All other acts of the will are of secondary importance compared with its action in the moral sphere, and here it fails. Obeying promptly the reason in almost all its other commands, it revolts and disobeys in this, and often the light of some good desire is still shining in the mind while the will has broken away and turned to the evil it hates.

We are so accustomed to these extraordinary paradoxes that we do not realize how amazing they are. If they happened in any other than the moral sphere, we could account for them only by madness. Yet no one can doubt that the moral life is the highest — no, we all recognize it as the essential life of man, to which everything else should be subservient.

What would we think of a man who constantly acted in direct opposition to his political convictions, or to his artistic or literary tastes? Or of a skilled and cultivated musician who loved the great masters but never played any music except of the most debased kind? Or of a man of refined tastes who always chose his friends from the most vulgar and ignorant? Or of one who constantly voted not only against his own party but against his own interests? And what would we say to such

people if, in excuse for their inconsistencies, they were to answer that they could not help it: "I cannot do the things that I
would"? We could only assume that such a course of action
was the result of insanity.

Yet in the moral life, such paradoxes are so common, such
everyday experiences, that we scarcely think of them, or if we
do, we speak of them as being only the inconsistencies that are
common to the frailty of human nature. But they are *not* common; they are in direct opposition to man's invariable rule of
action in every other department of life. There is nothing like
it in all his experiences.

Who could imagine a man constantly acting against his
own interests, his own desires, and his own tastes, hating the
things he did and still doing them? Who could imagine him
going forth with the full intention of pursuing a certain course
he had planned out and wished to pursue, and doing the very
opposite?

There is but one isolated department in man's nature where
the law of his action is altogether exceptional: where the intellectual and moral faculties refuse to cooperate, and the will
deliberately, often contemptuously, violates the commands of
the reason. It is like coming across a land where all the rivers
flow backward.

This, then, is the cause of the loss of that inner unity of
which every one of us is so conscious. Man is not at one with
himself. He is not sure of himself. He is not certain that he can
and will do what he wants to do; he is not master of the manifold resources that lie within his own nature, because he is not
sure of the loyalty of his own will. In certain things he is almost certain of its disloyalty, that it will betray his highest

interests and sell his birthright, as the son of God, for a mess of pottage.[31]

But why is this? If, in other things, the will and reason co-operate so well, what is the cause of this exception in the high-est region of the life of the soul?

St. Paul traces it to another conflict more deeply seated still. In a moment in which he is conscious of this revolt within himself, he cries out in amazement at his own inconsis-tency: "The good which I will, I do not, but the evil which I will not, that I do." He then proceeds to analyze and record his own experience.

He finds that these extraordinary moral inconsistencies arise because our nature is the scene of the constant strife of four forces, each struggling with the others for ascendancy over the soul. They are not impulses, or what we ordinarily mean by *passions*, which are violent and fitful in their action. They are forces acting as forces act under law.

And these four forces he calls "the law of the members, the law of the mind, the law of sin, and the law of the Spirit of Life."[32]

To these four forces, working with all the persistency and precision of law, he traces all that passes in the soul of good or evil; and to their conflict he traces most of the paradoxes. Now one force asserts itself, now another, and the will sways and is bent accordingly.

But if we look more closely, we shall find that these four laws work in pairs. One pair working together for evil and the

[31] Cf. Gen. 25:29-34.
[32] Cf. Rom. 7:23, 8:2.

other pair for good. "The law of my members brings me into captivity to the law of sin,"[33] and the "law of my mind" delivers me over to the "law of the Spirit of Life in Christ Jesus, our Lord, which sets me free from the law of sin and death."[34] The conflict is not directly between sin and holiness. There is a force, a law, that leads to sin, a tendency in the soul, not directly sinful, but preparing it for sin, which, if allowed to have its own way, will bring the soul under the dominion of sin. And there is a law that, if allowed to operate, will lead the soul held captive under sin, to its Deliverer, the law of the Spirit of Life, which sets it free from the law of sin and death.

Let us study a little more closely these four laws working for the ruin and for the salvation of man. The study will not, I think, be unprofitable in helping us to understand ourselves, our weakness and our strength, and in enabling us to see the central point in the spiritual conflict, where everything depends upon the practice of a steady watchfulness and self-discipline.

∞

The law of your members
prepares the way for sin

According to St. Paul, there is a law working in us resulting in acts and desires that are not in themselves sinful but prepare the way for sin. We know well enough what is definitely right and what is wrong, but there is something else, in itself neither right nor wrong, belonging to the debatable land, the

---

[33] Rom. 7:23.
[34] Cf. Rom. 8:2.

borderland between right and wrong. It is the region neither of light nor darkness, but of twilight. The soul that dwells under the law of this land will certainly end in passing over into the kingdom of darkness and of sin.

The heat of the battle does not, in fact, lie in the direct conflict with evil, but with things in themselves neither right nor wrong. The man who determines that he will not do what is positively wrong, but will do everything else he wishes, will find that, in the long run, he cannot stop short of actual sin.

There are in nature a multitude of phenomena apparently having no relation to one another, which a careful study shows to be all the product of the same law — the falling of an apple to the ground, the motion of the stars in their courses through the heavens, the weight of the atmosphere. And there are in the life of man a number of acts and words, of desires and inclinations, that, however independent they may seem, can all be brought under one category — the working of one steady and changeless law whose object is to bring him under the dominion of sin. This St. Paul calls "the law of the members." Let a man yield himself unresistingly to the control of this law, and he will before long find himself under the captivity of the law of sin.

We turn away at first in disgust and shrinking from sins that later on enslave us. We have not yet been sufficiently habituated to other things that relax the will and weaken the voice of conscience and lower the moral tone and prepare the way for a terrible fall. Little acts of self-indulgence, not one of them wrong in itself — the delight in the approbation of others, the full enjoyment of the gratification of the senses, the shrinking from hardships and the difficulties that life involves, the reliance on stimulants to whip up the tired powers of mind or body to meet some necessary strain, the dulling of pain by a narcotic, the turning from the uncongenial surroundings of domestic life to a friendship that is not in itself wrong but is fraught with danger — such things as these, not one of which in each separate act could be said to be wrong, have ended in the shipwreck of a soul. They all were the outcome of the constant working of that law of the members, which leads men captive to the law of sin.

It is against this law that the soul must keep up a constant warfare. Sin can gain a footing only when this law is allowed to have full play. The mortified and disciplined life alone will be able to resist the assaults of sin. There is, as St. Paul says, a constant and unceasing warfare between this law of the members and the law of the mind, before the law of sin can exercise its sway over the soul.

∞

The law of sin leads you to spiritual death

Sin, too, works by law. St. John speaks of sin as lawlessness: "Sin is the violation of law."[35] Yet these two statements are not contradictory. Sin is the violation of the law of the soul's true life, but sin has its own terrible law.

Disease is the violation of the law of physical health, because it sets itself to destroy those wonderful combinations and harmonies that are the result of life. But disease works by its own law. Every physician knows the stages of the progress of the fever, or the growth of the tumor or cancer. He knows the

[35] Cf. 1 John 3:4.

law by which they grow — a law that is opposed to the law of the well-being of the organism they have seized upon. In relation to that organism, they act in violation of law; in relation to their own development, under law.

It is the same with sin. Sin is the entrance into the moral life of man of that which is in deadly opposition to it, but which nevertheless works by its own law. The law of sin is death. It is the destruction of the moral life. Let sin enter into and take possession of the soul, and the soul dies. The will, although still in full possession of its strength for other work, is powerless to meet the assaults of sin. The reason, which, with wisdom, rules the whole nature in the ordinary affairs of life, becomes clouded and obscured in moral action. The powers of the soul become impregnated with disease; they refuse to co-operate for its well-being. They pass under the dominion of the morbid action of sin. The body once beautiful with the vigor and buoyancy of youth, laid low under the ravages of disease, robbed of every ornament of beauty, exhausted and overwhelmed with weakness, is but the image of the soul dishonored, discrowned, and defiled by sin.

Thus, once admitted and indulged, sin lives, grows, and develops by its own law. Its growth is like that of an organism that feeds upon the very life of the soul, absorbing its strength. Its life is the soul's death, its strength the soul's weakness, its growth the soul's decay.

We cannot bargain with it and say it shall go so far and no further. We can do only one of two things: kill it — cut it out as we would some cancerous growth — or leave it, and then it will grow according to its own law, not in obedience to any control of ours.

Abide by the laws of the spirit

We probably know nothing of that law, of the slowness or rapidity of the growth of some one sin that we leave to itself, until we find how deep its roots have spread, how exhausted the soul's life and how hideous and abnormal has been its development. Some organisms grow slowly, others with astonishing rapidity. And it is the same with this parasite sin. Some sins grow slowly and almost imperceptibly; the growth of such sins as selfishness, pride, and many others is so gradual that the conscience of their victims is not wakened or disturbed often until the roots are deeply embedded and the nature well-nigh enslaved. On the other hand, there are sins that grow and spread with a terrible rapidity, like the leaven that, in a few hours, spreads through and transforms the mass of dough.

Think of such a sin, for instance, as impatience if left unchecked. Think of how quickly it develops into anger, bitterness, and revenge. Think of how the imagination becomes discolored, giving the words and actions of others an utterly false interpretation. Think of how the victim of this temptation isolates himself more and more in morose and vindictive brooding, how the reason becomes deluded by the misleading of the imagination, and the once kindly heart is wrung dry of all affection and possessed by harsh and cruel hate. All the normal relations of life become strained or broken until the poor, deluded soul is left isolated in a bitter solitude, its hungry nature feeding on a poison that vitiates the springs of life.

He, then, who yields himself to the law of the members will find himself delivered over to the law of sin. These are the two forces, working with all the persistency of law, that cooperate for the ruin of the soul — beginning with the easygoing, pleasure-loving enjoyment of all that life has to offer, shrinking only from what is painful, and ending in the grim and hopeless slavery of sin.

Our Lord has drawn the picture: the prodigal going forth to a life of unrestrained pleasure with probably little knowledge or thought of anything positively evil, and ending with the cry, "How many hired servants in my father's house abound with bread, and I here perish with hunger!"[36]

∞

Let the law of the mind guide you

But there are two other forces that work with equal persistency and cooperate for the soul's welfare and deliverance: the law of the mind and the law of the Spirit of Life in Christ Jesus, our Lord. One of these is natural, the other supernatural, yet both equally work by law, and they work always together. As truly as the law of sin needs the law of the members to prepare for it, so does the law of the Spirit of Life need the preparation of the law of the mind. Obedience to the *natural* law of the mind is the preparation by which the soul is brought under the law of the *supernatural* power of the Spirit of Life.

The law of the mind is the law of the true self. The law of the members is the law of the lower self, and this is ever warring with the law of the mind. As one or the other of these gains the victory, one of the other two corresponding forces rushes in and takes possession.

There is, then, a law in constant and unceasing action whose object is to lift the soul up to all that is best in it — above itself into the supernatural. It is no intermittent impulse

[36] Luke 15:17.

coming now like a mighty wind and again sinking into stillness. No, it is a *law* always acting and always in the same direction.

Amid the din of conflicting motives that clamor for a hearing in the council chamber of the soul, one voice is always to be heard speaking for its true interests, against the sacrifice of the whole to a part, of eternity to time — one influence always acting for it. It is the law of the true self, the voice of conscience.

It is not an abstract law, nor an external law promulgated like the law of Sinai from without. It is above all things personal; St. Paul calls it "the law of *my* mind." It interprets all external law personally for the individual. There are obligations and duties that are binding on some and not on others, arising from vocation, position, religious training, and spiritual attainments; all these are taken into consideration. The law of the mind knows and gives due weight to the past, understands the capacity of the soul, its possibilities, and its destiny. It does not press upon one the standard of another, but interprets and applies all external standards to the individual. It will urge one to enter the priesthood and another to enter public life; it will lead one into the married state and another into the state of celibacy. It is the law of the perfection of the individual soul. Whatever the complications brought about by past sin, this law can point the way to liberty.

But, like all law, its strength and its weakness lie in the fact that it acts in the minutest details as well as in great things. The same law that controls the movements of the heavens controls the autumn leaf as it falls to the earth. And the law of the mind is ever acting in the smallest details of daily life.

With its prophetic vision, it sees the soul, already perfect, entering into the Vision of God. So that it may attain that end, it issues its command in some small and insignificant detail of duty. Its eye is always on the future, but its commands are in the present, as when our Lord, having foretold the martyrdom of St. Peter, turned to him and said, "Follow me"[37] — as though to say, "If you would be able to die the martyr's death, begin now by following me."

So the law of the mind works like the sculptor with his eye on the model and his hands upon the clay, molding it by touches so light, they are scarcely perceptible. We forget this prophetic character of conscience, and thinking its commands often are insignificant, being unfaithful in that which is least, we fail in the great result. If we would realize at each prompting of conscience, "This has more in it than I can see. It is the voice of my ideal and perfect self leading me on to perfection. This little detail is the next step toward perfection," we would be more prompt in obedience.

But shall we say, then, that to emancipate ourselves from sin, we need but to follow the leading of conscience? Surely not. We would find that very soon the commands of conscience were beyond our power to obey. What we need even more than light to know the way is strength to follow it. Conscience with its prophetic voice can lead indeed, but who can follow? "To will is present with me, but to accomplish that which is good I find not." The soul weakened, diseased, and paralyzed by sin can follow only a little way, with faltering steps and gasping breath.

[37] John 21:19.

It needs to be led to One who can heal its wounds and endue it with power. Conscience cannot save the soul from sin, but it can lead the soul to its Deliverer.

∽

Let the Spirit of Life lead you to Christ
The law of the mind brings the soul to its Liberator. And the Liberator of the soul is not a law, although it works by law. It is a Person: the Spirit of Life in Christ Jesus, our Lord. Striving to obey the voice of conscience, following it with halting steps, the soul finds itself handed over to a living Person who can flood its whole nature with quickening influences and the energizing hope that a person alone can give. This soul half-dead in trespasses and sins finds itself at last encircled in the sweet breath of the Spirit of Life, its tired and jaded nature healed and soothed by the balm of His presence, so strong and so gentle.

But even the Spirit of Life works by law. His action upon the soul is never lawless and capricious. He leads the soul through the law of the mind. Conscience is, as it were, a valve through which the stream of grace flowing forth from the Spirit of God floods the soul. If conscience is closed and the law of the mind violated, the stream is stayed; if conscience is open, the stream rushes forth in a mighty torrent, refreshing, invigorating, and uplifting all the powers of the soul. Then there is a kind of double action: the conscience itself hears the voice of the Spirit and becomes illuminated with supernatural light and sensitiveness, and so opens more promptly and more frequently, until, by the ceaseless flow of grace in which every faculty becomes steeped, the whole being is supernaturalized.

And it cries out in the joy of its deliverance and healing: "The law of the Spirit of Life has set me free from the law of sin and death."

But once more, the seat of the conflict lies not directly between sin and virtue, but, as the experience of all shows, and as St. Paul teaches, between the law of the members and the law of the mind. "The law of my members fighting against the law of my mind captivates me in the law of sin." Sin as yet perhaps dare not disclose itself. It sends forth its champion to exhaust the nature and tamper with conscience before it reveals itself. Behind the law of the members stands sin, behind the law of the mind stands the Spirit of Life, while conscience and the law of the members do battle. It is as it was of old. The Philistines sent forth their champion, and the people of God sent theirs, and Goliath and David did battle — David with his sling and stones but with all the forces of righteousness behind him, and Goliath with his giant strength and mighty sword and all the enemies of God behind him. If Goliath conquered, Israel would have been defeated; as Goliath fell, the forces of the Philistines fled before Israel.[38]

Thus, the great moral battle, whether the soul is to be ruled by sin or by the Spirit of Life, depends upon the victory of the law of the members or the law of the mind. About the trifling acts of self-indulgence or self-will against which conscience so vehemently protests, from the first waking in the morning when the law of the members cries, "Rest a little longer," and the law of the mind cries, "Arise and prepare for the work of the day," on through every hour, almost every moment of the

[38] 1 Kings 17:40-51 (RSV = 1 Sam. 17:40-51).

day, the tide of battle ebbs and flows. And behind these two combatants, whose conflict is over things so trifling that they scarcely seem to have any moral value at all, stand the two mighty powers of life and death, of sin and righteousness, awaiting the issue.

This, therefore, is the seat and center of self-discipline in that twilight land where the finest rays of light so blend with the darkness that the presence of the two can scarcely be detected.

Chapter Four

∞

Train your will

∞

The one supreme result of all the multitudinous activities that crowd and press upon human life is the formation of character. That which gives an intense interest to all that is going on around, whether in itself most eventful or most trivial, is the knowledge that all these things take their part in the shaping of character for eternity. These things are temporal, many of them momentary, but their effect is eternal.

> Machinery just meant to give thy soul its bent,
> Try thee and turn thee out sufficiently impressed.[39]

In a factory, we hear the clash and see the movement of the machinery, and to the untrained eye and ear all seems a bewildering and deafening combination of energy and noise. Then we are shown the work done, the result of all this activity — the woven texture of the tapestry. So it is with life. Man's character is forged by all the forces within him or outside of him that seem incapable of any moral interpretation and are designed, if they have any design at all, to force him to work: the needs of body and of mind, the motives that set the machinery

[39] Robert Browning, "Rabbi Ben Ezra."

of his nature going and tend to develop this power or that, the ambitions or passions that drive men to live the most strenuous of lives, or the lack of motive and will that leaves others to drift aimlessly where the currents and tides of other lives may lead them, the struggle for food, the lust for power, or money, or influence, and the vast multitude of people and things that claim men's time or interest or affection. All these things, everything great and small, most ephemeral or most lasting, everything that compels men to work or dooms them to idleness, everything that calls out a moment's interest or lays its grasp upon the heart, all these things, whether men believe it or not, or even think of it, have one supreme, one eternal result: the making of character.

∞

Your character will last beyond this life

We visit the scenes of ancient civilization, once the centers of intense activity, now silent and deserted; the records of human genius and ambition are all around us, yet the interest they awaken is not merely the interest of the antiquarian. There is a deeper and more human interest: these were the scenes of moral conflicts. These streets and palaces, these mighty temples and amphitheaters witnessed the struggle of conscience with human passion and sin, which we know so well, the struggle of the eternal with the temporal. The earthly end of those ancient civilizations was soon fulfilled, and they passed away; the thousand things that set the wheels spinning and kept them going have passed away. But the characters that were formed by them, whose shaping these silent streets and crumbling walls witnessed, remain forever. The things that seemed so important, that stirred the city to its depths and filled the streets with eager crowds, have passed like a storm and left no trace but upon the souls who bear them for eternity.

How little we realize this, the supreme purpose of life. As we think of men whose names are known in the social, political, and literary worlds and think of what they have done and how they have made their names memorable, we forget that the momentous question for them is not so much what they have done as what has been the effect of all they have done upon their own moral character.

It is not necessary that a man should realize this to make it so. Some realize it keenly, others never give it a thought, but it is true for everyone, whether he believes it or denies it. The veriest trifler who plays all his life upon the mere surface of things, and the materialist who denies there is any future life and who professes that moral distinctions are but the outcome of social instincts and hereditary training, are as deeply marked by life as the most serious and the most religious. No one can escape from it, whatever his creed, or, if he has no creed, whatever his philosophy of life, and even if he has no such philosophy, but lives only in the passing moment. Whether he ever pauses to think of what he is doing or not, the principle is the same for all: the one lasting effect of life is character.

As the noise and movement of the machinery of outward things sinks into silence, and the strain and pressure relaxes, each one goes forward into the silent world beyond, a lonely figure bearing upon himself the moral results of all he has passed through, for eternity. Man has *his* ends in it all, and they may be only temporal; God has *His* end, and it is eternal.

It is a strange thing, when we consider it, that of most of the great enterprises men undertake, what they would consider the mere accidents are often the most important results, and the enterprises themselves, their success or failure, are in truth but accidents. How many men realize that by far the most important result of the business they are engaged in, which taxes all their powers, mental and physical, is not whether it succeeds or fails, but whether it makes them honest or dishonest, thorough or slipshod, generous or mean toward the men they deal with — in a word, the moral effects upon them. Many a man has purchased success at the price of moral failure. Who would believe, if he were told, that the most important act in a day's work, in which great issues were at stake and all a man's resources were taxed to the utmost, was the self-control that was exercised, or the answer given to the supreme question that was being pressed home during all those hours of strain and tension, "Will you surrender principle for the sake of success?" The success or failure of life cannot be measured by material results; it must be weighed "in the balance of the sanctuary." Each of us is cast into the seething cauldron of the world with latent possibilities of good and evil, and we come forth well-shaped, strong, and purposeful, or crushed, misshapen, and demoralized.

We are thus led to look beneath the surface of all that is going on around us, and to see all as the machinery designed by God for the molding of character.

It is indeed a gigantic and massive machinery. But if we consider the vastness and complexity of the system He has formed for the well-being of the human body, needing countless ages of preparation and comprising not merely the earth but the solar system, and for all we know a great deal more; and if we realize how much more valuable the moral life is than the physical, it will not surprise us.

It will, moreover, encourage rather than discourage us. For in times of difficulty, when we are depressed with the slowness of our progress and the smallness of the results achieved, it will help us to realize the greatness of the task in which we are engaged to consider the greatness of the machinery we must employ.

The conquest of a temptation and the slow development of some virtue, the gradual building up of character, may be greater things than they seem to us. If it needs so extended and intricate a system, such a play of forces, and such a combination of people and things, to produce results that seem so small, it may be that I am mistaken in my estimate of their real value. If the world and all that is in it exists for man, and if man's work here is to overcome evil and to do good, then I am justified in estimating the value of goodness, which I can see but dimly, by comparing it with the magnitude and costliness of the machinery needed to produce it.

Think of the amount of energy of mind and body that is expended in one day in such a city as London, and compare it with the net results as seen by the eye of God, the results that remain and will remain forever — a little deepening of the lines of character in each person concerned, the threads of habit woven a little firmer, the voice of conscience somewhat clearer or less distinct, the will sunk a trifle deeper into its ruts or lifted a little out of them, and here and there some great victory for good or evil. The comparison of such results, as the only permanent ones, with all that it has taken to produce them, must force us to realize how different God's estimate of the true value of things is from ours.

∞

Many forces form your character

Life, then, is but the machinery by which character is formed. But in judging of a man's character, we judge it as a whole, with all its paradoxes and contradictions. It is a unit. We are led instinctively to lay stress upon some things and to pass over others more lightly, to bring together the good and bad, the weakness and the strength, and to blend them somehow into one harmonious whole.

One virtue does not make a good man or one vice an entirely bad man. The best men often have great faults, and the worst have their virtues. Sometimes we are surprised to find what good deeds a bad man will do, although we know that somehow they do not change his character. Peter denied our Lord, although he was a saint. Judas, with that vice that ruined him, had the qualities that would have fitted him to be an Apostle.

Indeed, there are not a few good men who have graver faults than other men whom we know to be bad. And there are men whom we justly judged to be bad who have never, taking deed for deed, done a thing in itself so bad as has been done by a man who is justly judged to be good. David's sin was in itself worse than perhaps any one sin recorded in the life of Saul.

When we say, therefore, that the end of life is the formation of character, and character is such a complex thing, how shall we judge it?

How can we compare men of utterly different dispositions? Here is a man of a hot, passionate nature, vivid imagination, and strong impulses. His blood flows like fire through his veins. Day by day he has to wrestle with temptations that another whose temperament is cold and phlegmatic knows nothing about. These two men look upon different worlds. What is a temptation to one does not awaken a desire in the other. What is sin to one, the other can do with impunity. Their temptations lie in different directions. There seems to be no common standard by which we can judge two such men.

How, again, is it possible to give due weight and consideration to all the circumstances of temperament, education, and religious training? Yet how can we judge character without such consideration? We must judge men by what they do, and we can only judge acts as in themselves right or wrong. A dishonest act is always wrong and must be judged accordingly. A murder is a murder, whether committed by a Christian in the streets of London or by a savage in the wild.

Yet when we pass from the act to judge the person who committed it, at once a multitude of considerations have to be taken into account that modify and influence our judgment at every step. An act in itself is easily judged as good or bad, but an act considered in relation to the person who did it is a very different thing. For then due weight has to be given to every circumstance of character, disposition, education, religion, and a hundred others. The man with inherited evil tendencies and brought up under every degrading influence can scarcely be compared with a Christian maiden brought up in a Catholic home and sheltered from childhood from every breath of evil.

∞

Remember the one measure
of every character

Yet when we say that the one supreme outcome of life is the formation of character, such a statement implies that there is some common bar to which all can be brought for judgment, some common standard by which all may be tested, whatever their temperament or training, whether they be savage or civilized, heathen or Christian, Protestant or Catholic. We must get down beneath all the accidents of life, to some common, all-embracing principle that applies equally to all, whatever their circumstances or nationality or religion.

Is there any such standard by which all can be judged? There surely is. For the moral result that the multitude of influences and forces that act upon any human life produces can be seen in their effect upon the action of the will in one special direction. Does the will strive after what the man believes to be right, or does it deliberately and consciously choose what he believes to be wrong? The answer that his life gives to these questions will enable us to form a very good estimate of his character.

And this test can be applied to all. Many of the standards by which we would judge men are inadequate; not a few are artificial. Here is one as wide-reaching as the human race and which goes to the very roots of character. By this test, all are brought to the same bar of judgment. It goes deeper than many of those questions by which men are apt to blind themselves to the main issue. No man will ever be judged by a standard he could not know: "He that knew the law shall be judged by the law; he that knew not the law shall be judged without law."

Nor will any ever be judged because he did not reach another's standard.

There is a great deal of emotional sentiment wasted by a certain class of people in describing the sordid and degraded lives of those who have lived from childhood in circumstances that shut them out from the possibility of better things, and they ask with bitterness why should such people be judged and punished for doing wrong that they did not know was wrong and for not living up to a standard that was impossible. The answer, of course, is simple: they will be judged only by a standard that *they* knew. Many of those upon whom such sentiment is wasted may be in fact better men and women than those who are pitying them. For they may be trying harder, while more severely handicapped, to live true to their own humble standard of rectitude.

We feel at once that, in judging character, everything else becomes of secondary importance compared with this. It is of the utmost importance to know the truth — there can be no more potent factor in life — but it is of little use to a man to know the truth if he has set his will deliberately in opposition to it. We can scarcely exaggerate the value of knowing the purpose and will of God. Yet the man who does not yet know the will of God concerning him, but longs and strives to know it, is better off than he who knows it and refuses to obey it. "He that knew the will of his Lord and did not according to His will, shall be beaten with many stripes. But he that knew not, and did things worthy of stripes, shall be beaten with few stripes."[40]

[40] Cf. Luke 12:47-48.

By this test, therefore, the whole human race can be judged; it goes deeper and reaches further and is more fundamental than the differences resulting from education, environment, heredity, or even the difference of religious belief. Under this test there is brought to light a cleavage in the human race that discloses a profound moral distinction between those on one side and those on the other. On one side are those who strive to do what they believe to be right; on the other, those who deliberately choose what they know to be wrong.

Some may have very crude and imperfect ideas of right and wrong, through no fault of their own, and their standards consequently will be very different. But the Catholic, in the full light of God's truth and with a sensitive conscience, and some savage fetish-worshiper in the heart of Africa, with the dim glimmer of an undeveloped and ill-educated conscience, each striving to live true to what he believes, come undoubtedly within the same moral category: both of these men are good according to their lights.

This, then, is what we mean, in the broadest sense of the word, when we speak of life as the training place of character and apply the saying to the whole human race. It does not lower our estimate of the value of religion or of the supernatural gifts of God — far from it. But it goes down to the root and foundation of character, upon which such gifts must act.

It is a solemn thing to look out upon the world of men in their manifold spheres of life, and to know that whatever they may be engaged in, in business or pleasure, in labor or in rest, sometimes silently and almost unconsciously, sometimes with effort and with tears, the will is gradually but surely turning in one or another of these two directions, and with an ever-increasing ease of choice and rapidity of motion, and that the whole character revolves with it.

But to constitute a moral act, the will must be free. No one can be held responsible for doing what he could not help doing. There is no character in a piece of machinery. An act is a moral act insofar as the will is free to choose one of two courses that lie open before it.

Yet it is undeniable that, while there lies deeply rooted in every one of us the ineradicable sense of freedom, there are at the same time many occasions in which this sense of liberty seems to fail us in the moment of some great temptation. We have it before and we have it after, but in the crisis of decision, we often seem to lose it.

I think most people have felt this. Looking forward to the temptation they anticipate, they know that they can resist, or, at any rate, that they can avoid it; and looking back after the sin has been committed, they are filled with shame and remorse and self-condemnation. But at the moment it seemed as if all the succors of their nature fell back and they were swept away in the strong currents of blinding passion.

And this is undoubtedly true. Who would be so rash as to assert that at any moment every man is free without impediment to choose as he wills? That the action of the will is unhampered by the past? That however often a man has yielded to a sin, at any moment the will is absolutely free from the power of that sin?

Which of us who has even the most superficial knowledge of himself would make such an assertion? No, such a doctrine could lead only to recklessness or despair.

∞

Choosing the good grows easier with habit

Every choice that is made develops a tendency to choose in the same direction. The more often we choose anything, the easier it is to choose it again. The law of habit reigns in the moral order as truly as the law of gravitation in the physical. The most difficult things become easy in time. It would be as difficult for a saint after long habits of virtue suddenly to fall into mortal sin as it would for a man living for years in habits of vice suddenly to become a saint. The law of habit presses upon the will, driving it into the channel it has cut for itself and making it more and more difficult to divert its course. The sense of power we have when, in some hour of calmness, we feel we need not yield is the assertion of the inherent liberty of the will. The remorse and self-condemnation if we yield is the revolt of the will against its slavery. The rising tide of passion or inclination that hurries it on in the moment of temptation is the pressure of the law of habit.

It would indeed be worse than misleading to tell a man who has long yielded to habits of sin that at any given moment he could, without constant prayer, vigilance, and strenuous effort, assert his liberty and never yield again. We can give him a better, more inspiring hope: we can tell him that he must *fight* for his liberty; that, as by his own act, he handed over this royal captive to the slavery of degrading and unworthy masters, he can fight and conquer its captors and set it free. We can tell him that habit can be conquered only by habit; that he must form good habits to conquer bad, habits of resistance to overcome cowardly habits of surrender. We can tell him that he is born free, not a slave; that this sense of his inherent liberty he never can lose: he can claim it and use it, or leave it to haunt him in his captivity, to his eternal shame and despair. We can tell him that it is not by violent and spasmodic efforts at self-assertion that he will overcome, but by steady and unremitting efforts at perseverance.

The law of habit can be conquered only by the law of perseverance. The will is under one law; it can be freed only by being brought under another law acting as steadily and persistently. "The law of the Spirit of Life . . . hath delivered me from the law of sin and death."[41] The bonds that bind the soul cannot be undone by any amount of random efforts to tear them off, however violent, or by any expenditure of muscular energy. They must be loosened knot by knot; the mad attempts to burst them only draw them tighter and leave the poor captive exhausted and despairing. The work of years cannot be undone in hours.

The prodigal who wakens to find himself a swineherd in a distant land cannot get back to his father's home, however much he longs for it, save by treading step by step the road he journeyed in leaving it. If he would hear his father's welcome and sit down once more at his father's table, the distance that separates them must be traversed every sorefoot mile. The hatred of his present degradation, the sense of the madness of his folly in leaving, the fierce revolt against his misery and against the citizen of that far-off country to whom he sold himself are of no use unless they brace him up to the great resolve: "I will arise and *go* to my father."[42]

---

[41] Rom. 8:2.
[42] Cf. Luke 15:18.

It is the failure to realize this that leads so many to despair: the deep-rooted consciousness of freedom in theory and its apparent failure in practice; the idea that we can at any moment easily assert our liberty in the face of long-rooted habits; that the sense of freedom needs only to be asserted to realize it in fact. It is not indeed a delusion, that sense of freedom; it is *the* great reality. But he who has sold himself into slavery must purchase his freedom at the full price he received for his degradation. There are few, if any, of those who have fallen victims to some degrading habit of sin who have not made efforts at some time to free themselves. They knew, like Samson[43] of old, their own inherent power, but they did not know the strength of habit and the power of sin. From time to time they would shake themselves free of their bonds and prove to themselves that, as they thought, they could at any moment assert their liberty; but they did not realize that their strength was gradually going from them and that the bonds with which they were being bound were stronger, until they awoke at last to the voice of the enchantress to find their strength exhausted and their freedom well-nigh forfeited.

The sensualist has his moments of reaction: he longs for purity; he knows he can be pure. In times of surfeit, when the strength of the passion is for the moment exhausted or satisfied, his better self comes forth and asserts itself. He is filled with a hatred of his sin and makes violent efforts to free himself, and the old habits fall back and wait. They know they can afford to wait. The efforts are too violent to last, and when he is exhausted and the nervous reaction sets in, these old habits

---

[43] Cf. Judg. 16:6-21.

quietly come back and bind their chains more firmly, and the dark despair of slavery settles down on him once more.

The law does not fear the violent outbreak of an angry mob. The law is stronger, however numerous the mob and violent its attack. What it does fear, and rightly fears, is organized revolt — law against law, organization against organization. Similarly, no momentary struggle, however determined, can overcome the firm grip of habit. It is only the steady, persevering discipline of the will in its captivity that can ever win for it its native liberty. No barrier, however strong, will stop the river flowing; you must divert its course into another channel. An idle man will not overcome his sloth by an occasional day of fussy activity, nor a miser his meanness by random acts of generosity, any more than a belated summer's day in November will stop the approach of winter.

∞

Once acquired, virtue is difficult for you to lose

This persistency of habit, which resists the random assaults to overcome it and leads so many to despair, is indeed the greatest source of consolation. It is the great source of the stability of character. If it is difficult to overcome bad habits, it is difficult to overcome good. The fact that the attraction to some sin persists in spite of all efforts to conquer it must encourage us to feel that it would be at least as difficult for temptation to assault or undermine in a moment a habit of virtue. If evil habits could be overcome by a few vehement assaults, so could good ones. There would be little hope of advance or stability. There would be no sense of security: the work of years might be destroyed in a moment.

But we know, alas too well, how the habits of the past cling to us, what a power of resistance they display. Well, this very difficulty to overcome the evil must give us a sense of security: a habit that will do such good service and become the very basis of character is worth striving to form.

No doubt good men have their moments of failure — moments, it may be, when under the force of violent temptation they sin. And although they must grieve over such failures, and grieve as only good men can grieve, yet surely they need not lose heart; the habits of a lifetime will not be destroyed by one failure. If they repent, those long-formed habits will reassert themselves. When a summer storm has passed and left behind it ruin and disorder, at once every constructive power of nature sets to work to mend and heal and remedy the work of destruction. And one storm of sin will not necessarily destroy all those positive habits of the soul that have been so carefully formed and developed in the past. Sin is indeed always bad, but we must not underestimate the power of good because we realize the power of evil.

Thus, as habits are formed, the character becomes established for good or evil upon lines that are not easily shaken. And the habit of choosing or trying to choose what is right builds the character upon the firm and stable line of moral rectitude, and one who so acts certainly is a good man.

∞

Choosing the good in small matters
will help you resist temptations

Everything, therefore, in which the will is called into action affects it in some way for good or for evil and forms the material for self-discipline, fitting or unfitting it for its great work in the choice of right and wrong. The hundred things each day on which we are obliged to come to a decision and make a choice — things in themselves of little importance — are the training ground of the will. In work, in study, in recreation, in the use of all those things that are necessary for our daily life, such as food and sleep, in the daily calls of duty, in the exercise of the powers of mind and body, in everything we have to do, in our relations with every person with whom we have dealings, by the Providence of God the will has to be exercised and trained, and it becomes weak or strong, free or enslaved, firm or vacillating, as a result. Each of these occasions may be small in itself and the decisions perhaps of little importance, but their frequency enhances their value and determines the result in graver matters.

We come forth from the daily round of work and pleasure to take part in the great moral conflicts that at once test and form us. But we shall find that the will has already its own marked characteristics, which were developed in spheres of choice that apparently had little or nothing moral about them. He who habitually struggles with everything — however harmless in itself — that tends to get too much hold on him, checking and mortifying his appetite, denying himself in things he likes, forgoing the use of that which he might legitimately have, so that he may not allow these things to encroach beyond their proper place, who trains his will to use the material things he needs only as means to an end, never allowing them to become an end in themselves, is not likely to fail under the temptation to unlawful pleasure. The victory or defeat in some sudden and violent assault of passion may depend upon whether we have practiced self-discipline in such small matters as food or sleep or little acts of self-indulgence.

Life will thus become in all its multitudinous opportunities a great school of moral discipline, preparing and training the will to be strong and firm, free to refuse evil and to choose good.

It is not, we must remember, upon the conduct of the soul in the moment of temptation that victory or defeat depends. It is upon its conduct in the lesser events of life. It is upon the constant struggle to keep the will from becoming enslaved to the mere tastes and inclinations.

The result of a great battle does not depend upon the moment's struggle, but upon the discipline and training of the troops in the past. Before a blow is struck or the first shot fired, the issue of the conflict is practically decided.

The conflict, therefore, must be unceasing; the opportunities of training the will present themselves every hour. Man is to be the master of all his powers and all his inclinations, and of all those external things God has placed in the world around him; he is to be the slave of none. He must wrestle with everything that tends to gain too much hold upon him until he has taught it its proper place, and then, in the hour of temptation, he will find that his will does not fail him. It is his attitude and bearing toward the small things that will decide the issue in those great moral conflicts upon which the welfare or ruin of his soul depends. "He who is faithful in that which is least is faithful in much";[44] and "He who despises little things will fall by little and little."[45]

---

[44] Cf. Luke 16:10.
[45] Cf. Ecclus. 19:1.

It is good to remember that if the will has been weakened and enslaved by sin, in the effort to recover and regain its former freedom, it does not stand alone. There is One with it to guide and to strengthen it. It is alone in its downward course. It has Another to help it to rise — One who will teach it the way, illuminating the mind with supernatural light, and endowing the will with divine strength. It could not rise in its own strength. Habits hold it in their iron grasp; it is in truth fast bound in misery and iron. Its own utter helplessness is its hope. Out of the depths of its despair, it must look to the Highest. In its utter ruin, it must look to Him who created it. Only He who made it can lift it up and restore it.

Yet it is no easy task. Its salvation does not mean any change of circumstance, or any outward change, or the removal of any outward difficulty. It must be restored, healed, strengthened, and illuminated within. This poor, broken, distorted thing must be mended and made fit to do the work of God, to overcome evil and to do good.

We often expect our prayers to be answered by the removal of obstacles that stand in our way, but that would not strengthen or restore us. Our prayers are answered by enabling us to overcome the difficulty; they are answered within. We do not expect merely that God will pity us and pardon us and admit us to Heaven, but rather that here on earth God will mend and heal us and enable us to do His work. The sinner must be not only pardoned but restored before he can enjoy the Vision of God.

And in every step of this restoration, there must be the act of the soul and the act of God — the will striving and God helping. "Apart from me," said our Lord, "you can do nothing,"[46] yet without our cooperation God can do nothing. The rusty wheels of our disused nature must be moved, and as they move, the unction of God's grace must flow over them. At first the motion is heavy grinding, clumsy, and agonizing, but as the sacred oil of divine grace flows over them, the movement becomes freer.

It is in action alone that the restoration can take place, and the will weighed down by the burden of the past gradually and by slow degrees regains its strength and elasticity. At first the task seems hopeless; the rust of long disuse impedes its every movement, and the law of habit holds it in its ruts. But as it struggles, crushed by its own weight, the dim light of faith grows stronger and gives birth to a joyful hope that stirs it to more persistent effort, and the sense of the divine Helper becomes clearer, surer, and more abiding. It finds that in every effort of the will there flows into it and over it a healing power that enables it to do what was once impossible. Through every channel of the soul, the voice of the awakening waters is heard after the long night of winter, and everywhere the tokens of returning life are felt, and the soul knows within itself that he who was dead is alive again; he who was lost is found.[47]

[46] Cf. John 15:5.
[47] Cf. Luke 15:32.

Chapter Five

∞

Control your thoughts

∞

One of the most remarkable characteristics of all forms of organic life is the power to adapt itself to the circumstances in which it is placed. It will endeavor under the most altered conditions to live, and, in order to live, it will resort to all kinds of contrivances, sometimes effecting such changes in its outward appearance that none but a trained eye could detect its identity. Yet with all these adaptations, it will preserve its identity.

Man possesses this power in perhaps a higher degree than any other form of life. He can find his home in any country, in any climate, under an almost infinite variety of conditions. He can live and adapt himself to circumstances involving the most violent contrasts and soon settle down and find the means of making himself at home. The change of the temperature by a few degrees of greater heat or cold will kill many of the lower forms of life. But man can pass from the sunny plains of the South to the ice fields of the North and is soon at home in his new abode. He who has been brought up in riches and luxury can adapt himself to poverty, and one who has never known a day's illness, when health is lost, in a few months settles down to the life of an invalid.

With all these external changes, there are corresponding changes in the person himself, no doubt, both inward and outward, but they do not affect his identity. The young man goes forth to the battle of life brave and strong and comes back aged, worn, and disappointed, bearing the scars of many a conflict and many a defeat, with powers of mind and body decayed. Yet through all these changes, the man is the same.

This power of adaptability is at once the hope and the despair of all who seek to do men good. It is the hope, because they know, however low a man may have sunk, if he will but struggle to rise, he can find his home and his happiness in better things. It is the despair, because they know, however high a man may have risen, he is capable, if he falls, of making himself at home in his degradation and his sin. There are on all sides men who have risen and are happy in a life that once seemed impossible and men who have sunk from all that was noblest to a life of shame, and still in their way are happy.

But man has other needs and another life beside that of his physical nature. He is something more than an animal and needs more than food and shelter. He may have every comfort and luxury that life can supply and be miserable, or he may be living in want and suffering and solitude and be happy. We can never judge a person merely by his physical surroundings. A healthy body and a plentiful supply of the good things of this world are not necessarily indications of a happy life.

For the life of man is above all things a mental life. He can never rid himself of the companions of his mind. He is not the mere creature of his outward circumstances. There are other surroundings that are far more intimate and closer to him than any external things, however nearly they may touch upon him. These things can but touch the surface of his being; his thoughts enter into the sanctuary of his soul. Lazarus in his outward wretchedness and squalor was in better company than Dives in his purple and fine linen.[48] The beast is wholly dependent upon what it finds around it. Man can live a life practically independent of most of these things. In the utmost solitude, he can gather around him a company of his closest and most intimate friends, and in the crowded thoroughfares of life, he can be alone with them. You may tell a man by his friends, but there are no friends so intimate as his thoughts. If you know the companions of his mind, you will know what kind of man he is.

It is not the sufferings or the consolations of life that directly affect character, but the thoughts that men call around them at such times. No external thing can in itself affect the inner life of the soul. Men are material; the soul is spiritual.

∞

Choose which thoughts to listen to

We often attribute to such things some moral characteristic, but in themselves they are neither good nor bad. The same things do harm to one person and good to another: suffering has been a curse to some and a blessing to others; poverty has closed the door of Heaven to some, and to others it has been the source of beatitude. The value of these things comes from the thoughts the soul calls around itself when it encounters such things. Some trouble comes into a person's life, and instantly there gathers around him, through the door opened by

[48] Cf. Luke 16:19-31.

that trouble, a crowd of thoughts, anger, rebellion, bitterness, and discontent and, at the same time, thoughts of penitence, acceptance, and the example of our Lord. The outward trouble has thrown open an unseen door into the spiritual world, and in flow this mixed crowd of thoughts, swarming around the soul and clamoring for a hearing. The soul must choose among them all which it will listen to and which it will reject, and by that choice, it rises or falls. One person chooses thoughts that heal, encourage, and strengthen him; another, those that stir him to bitterness and revolt. The morality lies not in the thing but in the person.

The contrast between the outward occasion and the inward choice is often startling: those things to which we are wont to attribute beneficent results produce not uncommonly the very reverse, and the things we consider evils are sometimes the source of great moral blessings. Or again, the same things produce evil in one man and good in another. Two people fall under the same calamity: it destroys the faith of one; it is the turning point in the life of the other and the occasion that first leads him to look to God.

We can never foretell the moral effect any combination of circumstances or events will produce on anyone, not even on those whom we think we know best. Men go down under circumstances in which we would have predicted they would rise, and rise when we expect them to fall. In fact, we cannot anticipate the effect of circumstances upon ourselves. We have occasionally been amazed to find that something to which we looked forward with confidence as a blessing has in the event proved very much the reverse. Such instances show that these external things are in themselves amoral — neither good nor bad — and if we look within ourselves at any such crisis, we shall see very clearly that the moral effect is to be traced to the thoughts they suggest and are the occasion of our choosing.

If we could look through the outward happenings in the world of sense to the results in the spiritual world in which the soul lives, our eyes would see strange sights: some event — it may be of little moment — a word, a look, a suggestion, the presence of some person, and the magic result. It seems to open an unseen door through which the strangest rabble crowd in and press around the soul, and a very babel of voices urge, entreat, and argue, quarreling and pushing forward for a hearing. And what a crowd! Some drawn from the lowest slums of the spiritual world, vulgar, lowborn, degraded, suggesting everything that is base and unworthy; others with clear, calm voices that pierce through the tumult, pressing some specious fallacy in well-clothed argument; others pressing forward, claiming a hearing as they have so often been heard before; and others again of noble form and gentle mien, waiting for a look, a word of recognition that they may drive this noisy crowd away and speak words of inspiration and courage.

The soul must choose, and what it chooses it will probably choose again and again, until that chosen thought gains the right of entrance, and closes the door to all others, and becomes the constant companion of the soul. And in every event, great and small, it enters and takes its place, instructing its pupil as to its meaning, interpreting it, explaining it — its hidden purpose, its power for good or evil — or misrepresenting it and making the good seem evil and the evil good, and gradually becoming master of its whole life, the molder of its character.

Indeed, it is true. These secret and unseen companions of the soul, intangible and volatile as they are, affect our whole view of men and things around us. The hard, substantial facts of life are interpreted by them; they become plastic in their hands, and change their appearance and coloring at their bidding. These phantom forms that rise out of the darkness and return to it again, colorless, impalpable, ethereal, that speak in inarticulate whispers and touch us with ghostly hands, are more real to us than the solid earth and the strong mountains. They can veil the heavens for us and take the brightness out of the sunshine and deepen the shadows at noonday or make the darkest day seem bright.

For they come from the same land whence the soul comes; they are of closer kinship than any material thing can be. And it is the mind that sees, not the eye. It is in the light that burns within that all outward things are seen. Amid the pleasant laughter and genial companionship of friends, some thought silently enters, holds up its lantern and casts its pale light around, and, seen in that light, all is suddenly turned to ashes, the voices lose their ring, and the laughter becomes hollow and cheerless. One thought in an instant has changed the whole scene from life to death.

It is thus in the thoughts men choose as their companions on their way through the world that the key to their interpretation of life is to be found. Different men view the same things in different ways. And the same men, in the course of a few years, alter their whole view of life. They have simply changed their companions on the road. Indeed, the breaking with one set of people and the forming ties of friendship with others of a different type is often but the outward evidence and result of a hidden and inward change of the more intimate friendships of the mind. How can one who has learned to take delight in thoughts that are low and degrading care any longer to associate with the high-minded? Who that has fought and conquered the evil desires that once enslaved him will still care to associate with the boon companions of his past degradation?

∞

Your thoughts color your experience

It is, then, in the light of our thoughts that we see and interpret the people and things around us. By a change of thoughts we change our view of life. It often seems to change the very people you encounter. A feeling of resentment sometimes has the effect of apparently changing the expression on another's face. And the same people look very different to the cynic and to the man of gentle and kindly feeling. It is undoubtedly true that the lines and shadows on the faces of those around us deepen or grow lighter under the changing thoughts within our own minds. We are astonished again and again to find how a person's face grows more attractive, becomes sometimes wholly transformed as acquaintance kindles into friendship and friendship into affection. Even the tones of the voice, even the meanings of the words that are spoken, have a different sound and receive a different interpretation from the changing moods of the person who hears them.

It sometimes seems impossible that some simple kindly meant words should be misunderstood, but to the ears of one person the voice sounds insincere, and the words receive the coloring and interpretation that comes from a mind filled with bitterness and antagonism. Surely there are not a few who look back upon misunderstandings, broken friendships, and some of the greatest mistakes in life — mistakes that it is now too late to rectify — and see clearly that the cause of them had no objective existence; it sprang wholly from their own subjective attitude of mind, which led to a false interpretation of words that were spoken and things that were done. Others who heard and saw and knew things as they were, sought in vain to explain, but it is the mind that sees, and the mind in its bitterness was out of tune with the world.

And so, again, a bad man sees evil everywhere, and a good man sees the world radiant with goodness. "To the pure all things are pure, and to the impure nothing is pure, but even their own conscience and heart is defiled,"[49] and because of the defilement of the heart, everything looks defiled. Two men go through the same streets, see the same scenes and people, yet the impression left upon the mind of each is different. The impression is the result of what their minds looked for.

No wonder our thoughts affect our judgment of men and things outside when they affect our judgments of ourselves. Many of us appear to ourselves to be wholly different people from what we really are. A few words overheard in childhood have been to some the beginning of a fantasy they wove about themselves that colored their whole conception of themselves through all the years that followed; and even some very rude awakenings to the reality have caused only a few hours of pain, until they could readjust themselves to the shock, and fall

[49] Cf. Titus 1:15.

back into their wonted thoughts. A parent's misconception of his child has often settled down upon him as a dark cloud that prevented him from ever knowing himself as he was in truth. Again, the constant companionship of some morbid self-conscious thought has hindered the usefulness and stunted the growth of many a life once full of promise. And many a man who has always regarded himself in the cold chilling light of self-depreciation and timidity has wrapped his talent in a napkin and done nothing for the world or for himself.[50]

∞

Your mind is easily molded

But if adaptability is the condition of life, and we can adapt ourselves with such extraordinary versatility to the changing conditions of our physical surroundings, we can do so to an infinitely greater degree to our mental and spiritual surroundings. There is a limit to the power of endurance of heat or cold, yet men can adapt themselves to the constant presence of thoughts that chill every hope and ambition and blight every noble desire. The same man may rise up to the contemplation of God, and live in the Communion of Saints, and find his joy only in those things that are pure and holy and of good report, and within a few years, he may turn from all this and choose for his companion the spirit of evil and delight himself in all uncleanness. He may do this and preserve his identity, adapting himself to the companion of his choice.

In two short years at most, Judas Iscariot had run through all the scale of spiritual experience from the highest to the

---

[50] Cf. Luke 19:12-26.

lowest. In but a few years, the narrow Pharisee with his exclusive views of Jewish privilege and his scorn for the Gentile world, broke away from the traditions and training of his youth and cried, "In Christ Jesus there is neither Jew nor Gentile . . . Barbarian, Scythian, bond nor free."[51] Henceforth, St. Paul rejoiced to see the God of the Jews as the God of the whole world, and the Messiah, not as a deliverer of one small people only, but as the Savior of the human race.

Yes, we always have to remember for good or for evil this almost unlimited power of the human mind to adapt itself with comparative ease to the presence of thoughts once unknown or hated. The constant presence of an uncongenial companion, the hostility of one whose will we have crossed, the feeling that we have a grievance — such things are often the occasion of thoughts that with terrible rapidity take possession of the mind and leave the impress of their presence upon the character.

There are many who have fallen from a childhood and early youth of spotless purity into a life of sin. There are men of business who have never diverged from the path of honesty until after middle life. There are men who knew nothing of the vice of intemperance until long after their characters and habits were formed and their position seemed well secured.

To such persons the memory must still be clear of the first approach of the temptation that was later to take so firm a hold upon them, of the recoil of the mind from it, with terror and repulsion, and yet with a kind of horrible fascination. It came again and again and stood at the door of the soul, awaiting its

[51] Cf. Col. 3:11.

admission with a kind of insolent assurance that if it waited long enough, it would have its way. By degrees, the mind was seized with a kind of tremulous excitement at its approach and bid it begone in tones of less confidence. It gradually became habituated to its presence outside the soul, feeling its influence, although never yet allowed deliberately to cross the threshold. Then it seemed to gain a certain strange influence over the various faculties, exciting an unaccountable curiosity and forcing them, as it were, to look at it, if only so that they might realize how hateful it was. At last it pushed open the door in a moment when conscience was off its guard and entered, and in an instant demoralized the whole household of the soul, loosened the passions, won over the imagination, and hypnotized the will. And although it was driven out and the doors barred against it, in that moment of its entry, it had made allies for itself, and now the passions and the imagination would loosen the bolts and the will itself would open the door for it. So it entered without let or hindrance, with an ever-weakening protest from conscience, until at last it gained possession, presided in the council chamber of the soul, cowed and silenced reason, and took the reins of government into its own hands.

Thus does the mind gradually become habituated and finally controlled by thoughts that once were alien to its whole training and habit.

We have indeed the power of refusing admission to them. In this matter we are certainly free to choose our friends. We are not responsible for the presence of a thought that we instantly repel. In the pressure of the crowd that is constantly coming and going, no doubt some thought occasionally passes the guard of conscience in disguise, and such can only be expelled the moment it reveals itself.

∾

Your mind can grow habituated
to choosing certain thoughts

But as time goes on, the power of choice becomes less free. The stream narrows and the currents become stronger. It is just as with human friendships: with advancing years, men make fewer friends, but cling all the closer to those they have. They become a part of their life.

In early youth, the manifold interests of life, the versatility of the mind, and the morning freshness that rests upon the world make life very complex: its currents flow forth in many directions. But as time goes on, it becomes more simple: the passions, the desires, the friends, and the interests become fewer, but all the more concentrated and intense. The many streams of youth flowing in deepen the channel and increase the volume of the river, and it is hard to change its course.

So it is with the mind: its choices have been made long ago. The claims of the thoughts that have been its companions for years are exacting, and they will not easily yield to a dismissal. They know the ways of the house of the soul; they claim the right of old friends to come and go as they will, and if they are barred out, they will force an entry. A thought that once could have been expelled easily and with scorn, dominates the soul now with insolent contempt and lords it over its cringing and frightened master. The elasticity and buoyancy of youth are over; the mind has no longer the rebound that once it had, nor the power of casting off its old associates.

"When thou wast younger thou didst gird thyself and didst walk where thou wouldst. But when thou shalt be old, thou shalt stretch forth thy hands, and another shall gird thee, and lead thee whither thou wouldst not"[52] — the silken threads of thought and act have woven themselves into strong ropes of habit that bind and shape the character.

> *Sow an act, reap a habit.*
> *Sow a habit, reap a character.*
> *Sow a character, reap a destiny.*

The character, therefore, will depend upon the thoughts. I am what I think — even more than I am what I do, for it is the thought that interprets the action. An act in itself good may become even bad by the thought that inspired it. A cup of cold water given in the name of Christ will be blessed,[53] while "if I should distribute all my goods to feed the poor, and if I should deliver my body to be burned, and have not charity, it profiteth me nothing."[54] A kindly person is one whose thoughts are kindly; a bitter person is one whose thoughts are bitter. A man who fights against the first approach of every evil thought is not likely to yield to sin in the hour of temptation, but one who has let his mind become habituated to such thoughts will find in the hour of assault that the citadel of his soul is betrayed. If Eve had not looked at the fruit of the forbidden tree, thought about it, and desired it, she would not have yielded. There is always an inner struggle and an inner yielding long

[52] John 21:18.
[53] Cf. Matt. 10:42.
[54] 1 Cor. 13:3.

before there is the outer, a yielding of the soul in thought before there is a yielding of the body in act. The startling moral collapse of someone well known and highly esteemed, which so often sends a shock of horror and amazement through the community, is only the last act in a long, silent, and unseen drama. The evil deed that showed the world it had mistaken its man really only disclosed the secret of his character. He did not become bad by doing the deed; he did the deed because he was already bad.

It is behind the veil in the silent world of thought that life's greatest battles have to be fought and lost or won, with no human eye to witness, no voice to cheer or encourage. There the strong citadel of the soul stands, a solitary outpost on the confines of the kingdom of God, and bears the brunt of ceaseless assaults. There the costly edifice of some seemingly compact and well-built character falls tottering to its ruin.

Clothed in these shadowy and illusive forms, the mighty forces of right and wrong do battle around the will, while the fair world smiles in the joyous sunshine and the merry voices of children are heard in the streets.

What a contrast there often is between the outward calm and the inner storm. The quiet life spent in the narrow routine of domestic duties, which seems so sheltered, so peaceful, so ignorant of evil — who knows? Inwardly it may be the prey to wild thoughts of revolt and ambition, hungering for the excitement of the great world that has been seen only in feverish dreams; or daily doing battle with naked passions that lift it to the heavens and cast it down to Hell. For no outward barriers can limit the soul or bar the door to the thoughts that seek to enter.

Control your thoughts

It is not *where* a person is that matters, but what he is thinking about. The whole edifice of the spiritual life may be tottering to its ruin and the enemy rushing in like a flood while the subject of this terrible disaster is on his knees and uttering the sacred words of prayer.

It is within, therefore, that the great battle of life must be fought; it is within, with our own thoughts, that we must struggle if we wish to see the world of men and things as it really is.

Our character, therefore, will largely depend upon the practice of that inner discipline by which we shall be enabled to gain control over our thoughts. Until we have done something in this direction, we will always have the feeling of insecurity; we cannot feel sure of ourselves, for we do not know where our thoughts may lead us or what they may induce us to do. The external restraint we put upon ourselves may give way any moment from the pressure from within. A storm of bitter thoughts will find vent in words, perhaps when we least desire it, or long-indulged thoughts of sensuality may in one unguarded moment lead to an act that causes exposure and ruin.

We must strive, therefore, to gain control over our thoughts, guarding the approaches of the mind, so that, amid the crowd that is constantly coming and going, none may escape our vigilance and, above all, so that none may be permitted to assert an independent authority.

∞
Controlling your thoughts requires prudence
Yet such a task, reasonable and natural as it seems, is not easy. There is the inherent difficulty of exercising this constant vigilance and of the fact that when we begin to take the

work seriously in hand, already the mind has formed its habits. We find that many a thought enters unbidden and refuses to go when ordered (or if it goes, returns almost before we are aware), and that some have enslaved the imagination and others the reason and others the heart. We find that these faculties revolt against the commands we put upon them and try to push aside the guards we set up and to open the door to them themselves. But besides all this, there is another difficulty, still greater and fraught with more serious danger.

There is the danger that arises from the exceeding delicacy and sensitiveness of the mind itself. It will not bear any unwonted strain. Any undue introspection induces a morbid condition that not unfrequently has more disastrous results than the lack of discipline itself. It has sometimes happened that an earnest effort to gain control over a mind long unused to discipline, suddenly exercised without due caution and discretion, not only defeats its own purpose, but brings on a mental paralysis that makes all concentrated thought impossible or so overstrains the machinery as to endanger mental balance.

Therefore, the effort to control the thoughts must be practiced with great caution. The desired results will never be gained by strained endeavors to drive away certain thoughts that have become habitual. I think it has been the experience of most of those who have tried this method that the thoughts definitely refuse to go — or that such violent efforts to banish them only give them a firmer hold.

You cannot, for instance, get rid of self-consciousness by trying, however hard, not to think of yourself. The thinking that you must not think of yourself only results in thinking of yourself all the more. You are, as a matter of fact, watching yourself all the time. The effort not to be proud will not necessarily lead you one step in the direction of humility. Humility is a very much more positive and vital thing than the absence of pride.

∞

Drive bad thoughts out with good ones

There is a better way: the positive rather than the negative way. Let not your mind be overcome with evil, "but overcome evil with good."[55] The emptying the mind of evil is not the first step toward filling it with good. It is not a step in that direction at all. If you succeeded in emptying your mind of every undesirable thought, what then? You cannot empty it and then begin to fill it with better thoughts. No, you must empty it of evil by filling it with good. Nature abhors a vacuum. You drive out darkness by filling the room with light. If you wish to fill a glass with water, you do not first expel the air; you expel the air by pouring in water. In the moral life, there is no intermediate state of vacuum possible in which, having driven out the evil, you begin to bring in good. As the good enters, it expels the evil.

Therefore, the effort of the soul must be to fill the mind so full of healthy thoughts that there is no room for others — trying not so much not to think of what is evil as to think of what is good.

The mind is ever working, never at rest. It will feed upon whatever food is given it. If it is given wholesome food, it will develop and grow strong. If it is given unhealthy food, it will

---

[55] Cf. Rom. 12:21.

grow morbid and sickly. If it is given no food, it will feed upon itself and wear itself out.

Mental sloth, inaction, a lack of any intellectual interest, leaves the mind open to become the prey of any thoughts that may enter, or turns it in upon itself. If it were kept in a healthy activity and its interests were constantly engaged, a great deal of mischief would be avoided. And this consideration should not be forgotten or ignored on the ground that any work of restoration or penitence can be done only by the grace of God. That is perfectly true; apart from Him we can do nothing. But the use of divine grace never dispenses us from the exercise of prudence and common sense. If you are ill in body, prayer and faith do not prevent the use of medicine and proper diet, nor do you need less such natural remedies for the ailments of the mind.

He, therefore, who wishes to overcome any habit of evil thoughts must do so indirectly rather than directly, trying not so much not to indulge in anger as to fill the mind with loving and kindly thoughts, meeting discontent by rejoicing in the will of God, self-consciousness by wrapping himself around in the presence of God — turning as promptly as possible to think of something bracing when he is conscious of the presence or approach of evil.

This, and the constant effort to keep the mind interested and occupied about healthy subjects that it can enjoy without strain or weariness will do much to recover it from the ill effects of the lack of discipline. It is a great matter to know how to give it relaxation without laxity and, by its studies and recreations, to prepare it for prayer and the more strenuous work of life. A mind that has a wide reach of interests and is constantly kept busy will have no time and no care for morbid thoughts. And the mind that is constantly fed on healthy and nourishing food will turn away from poison, however daintily served.

All this, it will be perceived, can be done with little introspection or self-analysis. It is based on the wisest of all systems: that nature works best if she is not too closely watched. A person who is always anxious about his health will never be healthy. Nature knows her own laws, and it is not good to interfere too much, even for the sake of putting them right. It is not an unknown experience that torturing scruples may take the place of mental laxity and a ceaseless introspection, which is the enemy of all freshness and spontaneity. We must take heed so that, in the efforts to overcome one evil, we do not fall into a worse one. We have to change the habit of the mind without giving it any undue shock, to keep it well in hand without seeming to watch it, to bring it under control without enslaving it and while seeming to leave it in perfect liberty. And to do this we need to have some confidence in its power to rectify itself if it is healthily fed and duly exercised.

But once more. If we would get our thoughts under control and discipline them to the best purpose, we would soon find that it is not with our thoughts alone that we have to deal. Thoughts are the product of the mind, as acts are the product of the body.

If a man desires to do the best work in his power, it is not merely the *work* he must consider, but the body by which the work is done. He may devote all his attention to the work in hand with very poor results, because it is the instrument that does the work that is out of order and needs repairing.

It is the same with the thoughts. As is the mind, so are the thoughts. Any defect in the mind discloses itself at once in the thoughts. A healthy, vigorous mind will produce healthy thoughts, and a diseased mind morbid thoughts. We often act like men who wonder at the badness of their work and try to improve it, but do not realize that the cause of it is ill health and that they cannot do better until they are stronger. And we wonder at our thoughts, that they are so unworthy, so feeble, or so little under control, but we do not realize that the fault lies in the unhealthy or untrained condition of the mind. It will never do better work until its health and training are improved.

∞

Bring your knowledge and love into harmony

Now, in the original design of God, the mind of man was one, all its powers cooperating for the well-being of the person and all guiding and aiding the will in its choice of God. As we look down into the depths of our being, we are conscious of dumb, blind movements of passion and feeling and excitement. We feel that there is a world of unexpressed desire, of inarticulate thought, that lives without any act of our own, wherein all the elements of life are striving for utterance. It is the seething, tumultuous spring of the soul's life.

We hear it like the voice of many waters; we feel it like the dumb pulses of a struggling life. It lives without any action of the will; we cannot tell where it comes from or where it goes. Then from this source, the stream of life goes forth in two directions: into the field of knowledge and into the field of love; on the one side, in search of all that is to be known, and on the other, toward all that is to be loved. These two streams were intended ever to flow together and intermingle. Into the hot currents of passion and feeling, the cooling waters of reason were to flow, tempering and calming them. And the cold stream of reason was to be warmed by the hot waters that flow from the heart. The heart was to kindle with its warmth the pale light of reason. And the light of the reason was to illuminate and control the blind impulses of the heart. Thus, love should be reasonable, and reason should be aglow with love.

But in our fallen nature, these two powers that were intended to cooperate for the well-being of the person tend to drift apart. The intellect becomes separated from the affections, speculation from practice, and pure reason from the moral life. The reason acts alone and as if it were sufficient to itself. Love uncontrolled and unguided by reason goes forth as a blind impulse, a passionate outburst. It loses luster, and its sullen fires smolder in the senses, consuming the whole nature.

We need, therefore, by constant discipline to bring these two outflowing streams together and to mingle their waters. Do not be content to know the truth; rouse your heart to love it. Do not be content with an unintelligent love of the beauty of truth; know it, study it, think of it. "Thou shalt love the Lord thy God with thy whole heart . . . and thy whole mind."[56]

Indeed, the devout Catholic will find in his holy religion the best of all schools of discipline. He will not be content with an ignorant delight in the beauty of his Faith, and he will find it scarcely possible for long to rest in a cold intellectual

[56] Matt. 22:37.

study of it, for here the heart sets the brain on fire, and the more he knows, the more he loves. Every new throb of his heart opens some hitherto unseen door into a deeper knowledge, and the warm and luminous stream of these intermingling waters bears him on their strong currents from faith to sight. For when these two separate, insincerity and untruth must be the consequence, and where one or the other controls the mind, it will fail to see things as they really are.

It is a terrible thing to let the heart live its own life separate from the intellect; to know what is true and to love what is false; to feed the mind upon one thing and the heart upon another; to let the life of the heart drift into a different channel from that of the head — more, to let it live upon that which the head condemns. Such a divorce between the two powers, which should cooperate and help one another, leads finally to a double life of falseness and insincerity in which each goes its own way, and the cold and loveless intellect and the passionate and unreasoning heart rend the inner life in twain. Who can trust the judgment of such a mind? Is it any wonder if its decisions are misleading? What must be the condition of the inner life of one in whom the radiant forms of truth and the base desires of uncontrolled passion have come to terms and live peacefully together?

But again, if one of these two sides is unduly developed to the detriment of the other, the mind will suffer in consequence and will fail to gain the full knowledge of the truth. For the heart is needed even for the acquisition of knowledge. There are secrets that can never be disclosed save on the condition of love. The poet has a revelation to give that is wholly unknown to science. Love opens the eye to see what the unaided reason could never see or, if it did, could not understand. No one ever knew another thoroughly who did not first love him.

It is not that love merely transforms and idealizes; it reveals. "He that loveth not, knoweth not God."[57] If, therefore, the intellect is unduly developed to the neglect of the heart, the intellect itself will find there are certain fields of knowledge closed against it, to which the heart alone can supply the key.

And certainly one who has lived the life of the affections to the neglect of the intellect will never experience the highest enjoyment of the affections. For there is such a thing as intellectual love — a love that springs from and blends with knowledge; such a love as that which we can imagine a man of science who is also a poet to have for nature; such a love as our Lord commands us to exercise toward Him when He says, "Thou shalt love the Lord thy God with thy whole mind."

We should therefore discipline ourselves by the cultivation of that side in which we are defective, stirring our hearts to love what we know — "while I was thus musing, the fire kindled";[58] or forcing our minds to acquire deeper knowledge of what we love, so that, the whole mind being brought to bear upon the whole truth, as a flawless mirror, it reflects it as it is.

∞

Let memory and imagination guide you

But once more, the soul stands midway between the past and the future. The light of the present falls for the moment upon it, but only for a moment; in an instant the present

---

[57] 1 John 4:8.
[58] Cf. Ps. 38:4 (RSV = Ps. 39:3).

becomes the past. The past sinks into the darkness and cannot return; the future is shrouded in darkness and cannot be foreseen. But for the light of the passing moment, the soul's life would seem to be surrounded on all sides with darkness, like the bird that flies through the lighted chamber coming from the night and returning to it again.

Yet man must look backward and forward. He cannot live in the fleeting present. Out of the past come the experiences, the warnings, the lessons that are to guide him, and if he cannot see some little way into the future, he will stand trembling upon the edge of the light of the present, too timid and fearful to press on. He must look backward and forward if he is to make the best use of the moment. The currents of the past must press him forward; the eager anticipations of the future must draw him onward.

God has given him two great powers: one that looks backward into the farthest past and stores up its treasures, the other that presses forward and lifts the veil overhanging the future. These two powers are memory and imagination.

Without memory, we would gain no experience, acquire no knowledge. We would have momentary visions of swiftly passing scenes, rising for an instant into view and plunging into the darkness. Life would be a bewildering scene of kaleidoscopic changes, each vision isolated and disconnected. We would be like someone hurrying through some strange country at breathless speed, never able to pause and consider and draw lessons from what he sees, for each moment's vision stands alone. By memory we turn the great searchlight of the mind upon the past and dispel the darkness; and wherever the circle of that light is turned, the past is seen again, not, it may be, in the warm colors of the living day, but in the pale yet penetrating light in which memory clothes it. By memory we can accumulate the wisdom and experience of past ages, and store our mind with knowledge and daily increase its treasures. And the voices of the past call to us in the chamber of the memory with words of warning, encouragement, and instruction, urging us forward, holding us back, and pointing out to us the way.

By imagination we can peer into the future. We can see the goal at which we aim, the rest for which we labor. We can make the unseen more real than the seen, and things that are not more real than those that are. We can anticipate events long before they come to pass, and see visions in a flash that take years to carry out and realize. Without imagination the hands fall heavy at the side, the feet are weighted with lead, and the mind gropes forward through the darkness and stumbles at every step. We light the torch of the imagination and walk with steady step and kindling eye into a future bathed in its light.

Thus we can look backward and forward and, in the wisdom of the past and the anticipation of the future, tread with head erect and wide-eyed vision the path that is set before us.

∞

Do not abuse memory and imagination

Yet these two great powers given us by God to aid us in our earthly sojourn can be abused, and become not the spring of progress, but a source of stagnation and failure.

It is possible to use both memory and imagination as instruments of self-indulgence, as ends in themselves, and not as means to help the soul onward.

There are those who find in the memory no stimulant to action, no lesson or warning for the present, but a chamber of pale dreams and ghostly forms where they spend listless hours of sadness or regret, and from which they come forth unmanned and spent and incapable of action. They live in the past, not in the present or future. They live in it, not to learn any lessons but to indulge themselves, breathing in those faded perfumes which, like narcotics, deaden and stupefy the powers, unfitting them for the work of life.

Who that has passed middle life does not know the danger of turning the chamber of memory into a place of shadowy dreams and vain regrets and weary longings — where the heart exhausts its strength by the passion of its yearning for what can never be again, and the mind grows weary in thinking what it *might have done*, and old deeds buried in the years rise and lift accusing eyes that make the heart grow sick with despair? Who does not know what it is to come forth from such memories unmanned and exhausted, and feeling their ghostly and unhealthy shadows rob the very sunshine of its sweetness?

Imagination, too, can be abused and become a source of self-indulgence and a hindrance rather than a help to life.

It is the greatest of all the powers — the creative faculty, the power of vision — by which things are first seen and then made real. It saw the world's great buildings before a stone was cut in the quarry. It has heard music that the skill of the musician has sought in vain to reproduce and seen forms of beauty of which the greatest works of art are but a faint shadow. Its visions have led science on to its great discoveries, anticipating with giant strides the slow processes of the reason. It has planned the battle and secured the victory for the great general before the first blow was struck. It has anticipated every forward step that the human race has ever taken, painting the vision in vivid colors before the eye of the seer, who, having seen, urges men forward to make the vision real. It has stood from the dawn of our race beckoning us onward, like some great magician filling the air with sights and sounds that seem like dreams, but stir men's minds to thought and their hands to action.

So, if we draw from the treasury of the memory the wisdom of the *past,* imagination urges us ever *forward;* it is "the sting that bids nor sit nor stand, but go."[59]

And this great power that transforms life and creates new worlds can be, and is by not a few, prostituted to be the source of idle amusement and self-indulgence. There are many who do not try to make real the creations of their imagination or use them as a stimulant to action, but who turn to them from the realities of life; who live in a dreamland of their own fancy that becomes to them more real than the facts of life itself; who use this great gift as the handmaid of their vanity or sensuality and fly for refuge from the demands of life into a world of unreality and dreams. The power that has acted as one of the greatest stimulants to urge men forward is used by such people as a drug under whose soothing influence they are content to dream away their existence.

It is the office of mental discipline to recover the powers of the mind for the work for which they were given and to restore to them their proper balance and unity. This can be done in its

---

[59] Browning, "Rabbi Ben Ezra."

fullness only in the service of God. With heart and head united, and each helping the work of the other; with the roots sunk deep into the past, and life enriched and urged forward by all the wisdom and warnings of memory, and imagination lifting its burning torch and making vivid and real what has been revealed to faith — the action of the will will be invigorated, and the soul will press forward to the prize of its high calling in Christ Jesus, our Lord.

Chapter Six

∞

Strive for balance

∞

Most of the heresies that have opposed the Church in her progress through the world have arisen from the undue pressing of one side or one part of the truth. For the truth of the Christian Faith can generally be stated in the form of a paradox. And any failure to keep perfect balance and proportion in these statements results in error. The history of the struggles of the early ages is the history of the wonderful instinct with which the Church ever preserved the mean between the extremes toward one or another of which the human mind tended in the definition of the doctrines of the Faith.

In the definition of the doctrine of the *Trinity*, on the one side, were the Sabellians, who, in their effort to preserve the idea of the unity of the Godhead, sacrificed the threefold Personality; on the other, the Tritheists, who pressed the doctrine of the Three Persons into that of three separate and distinct Gods. Between these two stood the Church, preserving the truth and rejecting the extremes of both. The Godhead is one in three Persons. "The Father is God, the Son God, and the Holy Spirit God, and yet not three Gods but one God."[60]

[60] Cf. Athanasian Creed.

Christian Self-Mastery

So, again, in the doctrine of the *Incarnation*. The mind faltered before this great doctrine and bent now toward one side, now toward the other. Some, according to their natural temperament or their sense of the needs of man, pressed the Godhead of Christ to the injury of His perfect manhood. Others sacrificed the perfection of His Godhead to what they believed essential to His manhood; or yet again, so defined the union of the Godhead and manhood as to destroy the unity of His Person.

But amid all these controversies that spread over several hundred years, ranging from gross heresy to the nicest and most delicate overstatement or understatement of a truth, the Church ever kept the balance between the extremes of the contending parties, and taught that "Christ is perfect God and perfect man," and that the union was effected "not by confusion of substance, but by unity of Person."[61]

So, again, with the doctrines of *human* life. Some, looking upon the nature of man, have felt most keenly its inherent badness; others, its inherent goodness. But the Church, recognizing fully all the evil and all the good that is in man, taught that his nature is neither wholly bad nor wholly good; that he is a being created in the image of God, but fallen, and that without God's grace he cannot attain to his perfection.

Again, in regard to man's *spiritual* life. There have been those who have taught that man's greatest act is to be still and to leave God to work within him — that man can do nothing; God must do all. On the other hand, there have been others who, feeling the intensity of their own struggle and little sense

[61] Ibid.

of supernatural help, have taught that man must fight as best he can his own battles. And the Church, recognizing what was true, and rejecting what was erroneous and exaggerated, in each, taught the truth in the great paradox of St. Paul: "Work out your salvation. For it is God who worketh in you."[62]

∞

Do not develop only part of your soul

There is the same danger of this pressing of part of a truth in the *practical* life. Man has many sides to his nature, and his conscience must take them all under its care. If he neglects part, he will find that he has injured the whole, for all are a part of the one person. It is true in more senses than one that "the eye cannot say to the hand, I have no need of thee."[63] Every member of the body must be used for the welfare of the whole organism. And every side of life must be used if a man is to be at his best.

Indeed, if anyone sets himself to develop merely one side, he will find that he fails to perfect even that side, for it needs many things that come to it from other quarters. One man determines to develop the social side and altogether neglects the religious, but he finds in time that the social side fails in its perfection through the lack of just those things that religion alone could give him. Another neglects the social side for religion, and he soon finds that his religion becomes fanciful, fantastic, and deceptive, unless it is brought in contact with the hard facts of human life and experience. Another determines

[62] Phil. 2:12-13.
[63] 1 Cor. 12:21.

that he will give his life to the training and development of his reason alone, but he learns, perhaps too late, that he is not merely a reasoning but a moral being, and that the reason isolated and separated from the rest of his nature suffers vengeance at the hands of those powers which, as its fellow workers, would have helped and perfected it.

There is the same danger in the struggle with sin and the effort to form virtues. Many people who set themselves to conquer one fault and give their whole minds to this will find, if they are not careful, that they have only fallen into another.

For virtue cannot thrive in the narrow soil of one department of the soul's life, unnourished by the streams that should flow into it from all sides and unpruned by the hand that watches over and labors for the enrichment of the whole. Every Christian virtue has more sides than one and is a more complicated and delicately balanced thing than we imagine. It has to look, as it were, toward God and toward man; toward the person in whom it dwells and toward others; toward itself and its place in the soul and its relations with other virtues. It has to be tended in its growth by the intellect as well as by the will and affections, and has to endure much severe pruning at the hand of reason. It must be able to live in the open and bear the hard dealings of the rough world, and it must grow in the silence of prayer and the presence of God.

There may be such a thing as the overgrowth of the one virtue to the crowding out of others that are equally or perhaps more necessary. Or, on the other hand, we may develop a virtue in one department of life to the neglect of all others. It is not uncommon to find a man very different in his domestic relations from what he is in public life. There are not a few who are thoroughly truthful and honest in all the concerns of life except in the conduct of their business. But a virtue is not a Christian virtue if it is exercised with exceptions. It must have its roots in the *person* and spread through every department of the soul's life.

In the effort to conquer our faults, therefore, we have to be on our guard against the danger of being one-sided. For the very virtues we may be striving for are not so simple as they seem, and the materials of which they are formed, if not mixed in exact proportion, may produce not a virtue but a fault.

Humility is the perfect blending of the very highest and the lowliest thoughts of oneself. The humble man is conscious at once of his own nothingness and of his exaltation as God's creature, whom He would unite to Himself. And he somehow contrives with the deepest sense of his own unworthiness to maintain a dignity that wins respect. If he leaves out this self-respect, his humility is not true humility and ends in self-degradation.

Meekness is the blending of gentleness and strength — a strength that has been won by victory over self and passion, and a gentleness that shows that this victory is the outcome of no harshness and bitterness toward self or the world, but of love. Test true meekness by the severest trials to which it can be put, and you will find in it no flaw of weakness or harshness, but a dauntless courage of the loftiest kind and an inexhaustible gentleness.

So with charity. Christian charity is not a blind disregard of facts, a refusal to see things as they are, a condoning of the sins of others. It is the love of the sinner springing from the love of God, which necessitates the hatred of sin. There is a great deal of spurious charity in the world, making excuse for sin or ex-plaining it away, devoid of strength and virility, and often mixed with insincerity and unreality. True Christian charity blends in perfect proportion justice and love.

Thus, we might go on and see how every virtue involves the balancing and blending of characteristics that seem at first sight almost opposite, and thus embrace the whole many-sided nature of man and keep him exact and well-proportioned. There is more truth than we realize in the saying "Every vice is a virtue carried to extremes."

∞

Balance your independence with
your dependence on others

Now, for the training of our character here on earth, each of us has two spheres of discipline activity. We have our life and duty to ourselves, and we have our life in its relationship to others. A duty is a debt, something that we owe. This is not of our own making; it is a law under which we find ourselves placed — a law, indeed, that we are free to keep or to break, but if we break it, we must bear the consequences; and the im-mediate consequence is some moral loss to ourselves.

I cannot with impunity violate my duty to myself for the dearest ties of friendship, or the closest bond of kinship, and I cannot violate my duty to others for advantage to myself. The law of self-development can never be — although it some-times may seem to be — in conflict with the law that regulates my relationship with others. There is a sense in which we must never sacrifice ourselves for others, any more than we may sac-rifice others for ourselves.

God has so ordered it that the welfare and perfection of the individual is bound up with others: "It is not good for man to be alone."[64] Except in the case of a very special and marked vocation, man is meant to be and to live as one of a multitude, bound to it by many ties. Yet at the same time, he must guard and shield his own life so that it does not lose itself in others. Let a man isolate himself from others, and he soon becomes eccentric and morbid and loses the true perspective of things and gets a distorted view of life. Let him throw himself unguarded into the crowd, and he quickly loses his own individuality and becomes soft and plastic. From the moment in which consciousness awakens, on throughout the whole course of life, our duties to others and our relations with them become more involved and far-reaching, and our duty to self more peremptory and exacting.

Consequently, in the life of every man whose character is developing along its proper lines, there will be two apparently contradictory characteristics: dependence and independence. These two must blend and harmonize in due proportion as life advances. The man who is recklessly indifferent to others bears the mark of failure stamped upon him, and he who is wholly dependent loses all individuality and all power of influence in the world. This is true of those who are naturally strongest or weakest, and it applies equally to women and men.

It is a constant surprise and delight to find these two characteristics coexisting often where we least expect it. The strong man whose most prominent characteristic is individuality, leadership, the power to stand alone, in proportion as he

[64] Gen. 2:18.

is influenced by religion, will be found to have a surprising consideration for others. There is in him no reckless indifference to the men he has to deal with; he does not glory in isolation and trampling upon their opinions, but he feels and recognizes their rights. As we get to know him better, another side of his character discloses itself, rich with the ties of many friendships and a broad toleration, and open to many influences that soften and widen and enlarge his whole nature.

Who does not know such men, and feel the contrast between them and those who delight in differing from others and in forcing their own opinions and in standing apart and alone?

On the other hand, how many who seem weakest and most easily influenced show a strength that can resist the world when it comes to a question of principle?

It is the harmonizing of these two apparently opposite characteristics, balancing one another and correcting one another, that produces such exquisite and delicate results. The roughness and independence that are the natural danger of the strong man give place to a considerateness, a readiness to be influenced, and a delicate sensitiveness that is all the more attractive because of its unexpectedness. And the most dependent and naturally weak is protected from colorless insipidity by a moral strength that rounds the character off and saves it.

A healthy life, therefore, should have its roots spread deep and wide in the soil of the human family, and its whole human nature open to the manifold interests and influences and associations of the world around it. At the same time, it should possess an ever-deepening sense of the claims of God, of conscience, and of truth, so that it never likes to part company with its fellowmen, but is strong enough to stand against the whole world at the command of duty.

Now, this dependence of our nature upon others, by which we are meant to be humanized and kept from going off into eccentricities of thought and action, is secured for us in many ways and, among others, by the fact that, in the two strongest and deepest feelings in our nature, we cannot stand alone.

∞

Know how powerfully others affect you

Man was made for eternal happiness, and if he refuses it, he will have eternal sorrow. Joy and sorrow, therefore, are no superficial things; they are the heights and the depths of our nature. It is a strange thing that whatever else each of us can keep to himself independently of the whole world, no man is independent in his joys or his sorrows. The veriest stranger whom we have never seen before can for a moment cloud our happiness or cast a ray of sunshine through the darkness. The passing of a fellow creature in the street, a face seen for a moment in a crowd, can haunt us for days with a feeling of distress. Anyone can rob me of my joy for a moment at least; anyone can give me some momentary passing pleasure. A word, a look, and I bear about with me for the whole day an open wound. Or again, some kindly word of encouragement opens a spring of joy that makes the whole world look brighter while it lasts.

I doubt if any combination of mere circumstances can give us such happiness or sorrow as one human being can give. No bodily pain is half so acute as the pain that one man can inflict upon another, and no happiness is so deep as that which comes from human fellowship. The presence of one person can destroy the happiness that every circumstance of life combines to produce, and the saddest and most unhappy surroundings can be forgotten or transformed by the presence of a loving friend.

What power lies in personality! All the events, surroundings, consolations, and sufferings of life sink into insignificance before it. A little child can do more to gladden his mother's heart than everything the world has to give her. Two human beings wrapped in one another's love can see the world go to wreck and ruin without a sigh. And truly, "the light of the whole world dies when love is gone." Yes, one person has more power to give joy or sorrow to another than all the wealth and influence in the world. The heart cannot rest or find its satisfaction in these things; a *person* steps in among them and changes them all. The presence of an unloving husband or wife has often turned all the wealth and material comforts and social enjoyments the world has to give into ashes. And pinching poverty and constant ill health and grinding work have been transformed by the presence of love.

It is undoubtedly true that each of us, men and women, irresponsible and thoughtless as we often are, hold within our hands the happiness and sorrows of others. We cannot help it or escape from it. The power is in us inalienably almost from birth to death — in us, because we are persons — and we are responsible for the use we make of it. Indeed, so mysterious is this power that the very presence of a person who does not realize his responsibility is often the source of the keenest pain of all. What greater misery is there than to be linked to another who ignores you, who shows neither interest nor concern in your doings, neither blames nor approves, neither loves nor hates, but freezes you up by the blight of an absolute indifference. It would be easier to bear aggressive dislike.

The failure to exercise the power to give happiness to others is not merely negative in its results; it is the source of the most positive suffering of all. Thus there is no escape from the responsibility involved in the possession of this power. Not to use it where it is due is to destroy all happiness.

Strange power, indeed, to be committed to such weak and unworthy hands; yet there could be but one thing worse: that none could interfere with the joys and sorrows of others. We might envy their happiness and pity their sorrows, but we could not help them. It would be a world of isolated individuals wrapped in inviolable selfishness; each must take care of himself and the world must go its way.

Now, this power of giving happiness and sorrow to others springs mainly from two great passions that exist in every member of the human race: love and hate. There is no one without them. They are the strongest and deepest powers we possess. By these, the world is ruled. It is doubtless true that every great movement depends upon thought; the conflict that effects a great revolution is a conflict of ideas, and the revolution is the victory of one set of ideas over the other. But the masses will not be moved by philosophical conceptions; they are moved by passion, and philosophy has to be translated into the hot language of feeling before the multitude is stirred. The crowds surging through the streets of Paris on the eve of the great Revolution knew little and cared little about the speculations of a dreamy philosopher; those ideas had come to them in the practical form of paying off old scores.

Cold speculation was on fire with human passion, and the face of society was changed.

Love and hate, then, are the most universally felt and the most easily excited of all the powers of our nature, and it is mainly by these that the happiness and sorrows of others are affected. The presence of love, wherever it is, in however obscure a person, will at least do something toward lightening the sorrows and securing the happiness of others; and hate equips the most insignificant with an instrument that works sorrow.

∽

Hate and anger are essential
elements in the spiritual life

Yet both of these are, equally, divine gifts. "Love is of God," says St. John, "and everyone that loveth is born of God, and knoweth God . . . for God is love."[65] But love involves and necessitates hate. God hates evil, and such hatred must be an essential attribute of God. The power of hatred, then, is as truly a divine gift to man created in the image of God, and as necessary an element in the Christian character, as love is. "O ye that love the Lord," said the psalmist of old, "see that ye hate the thing that is evil."[66]

He who is incapable of hating is so because he is incapable of loving. The intensity of the power of hating will always be in proportion to the power of loving. We feel instinctively that a man who cannot hate, whose anger and moral indignation

[65] 1 John 4:7-8.
[66] Cf. Ps. 96:10 (RSV = Ps. 97:10).

can never be roused, is a poor creature. A strong man will always be strong in his likes and dislikes. All this may — and, in fact, generally does — work evil. Yet it is not essentially evil, but good. Love can work evil as truly as hate can, for it may be exercised on an unworthy object and in a wrong way, but it is not therefore an evil thing, and no more is hate. They are both part of the equipment of man's nature. They work together, they grow together, and together they die.

The instrument with which hatred fights its battles is anger. Anger, too, is an essential part of man's nature, as it is also a divine attribute. If man is to be Godlike, created as he is in His image, he must be like Him in this, too. We read of "the wrath of God."[67] We are told that our Lord "looked about upon them with anger."[68] It is an apostolic precept: "Be angry, and sin not."[69] Yet, if I were to ask what has hurt the affections, broken the hearts, and ruined the homes of men more than perhaps anything else, you would tell me that it was anger.

Yet no man is worth the name of man who does not sometimes get angry. Indeed, the anger of no one is perhaps to be feared as the anger of the just and good. How is this?

Anger is the sword that God puts into man's hand to fight the great moral battles of life. The more he loves God, the more he will love good and hate all that assaults or tries to undermine good. And, as he was created to love God, and all else in God, so he was only to hate all that was opposed to that love. Into the hands of hatred was given the glittering and

[67] Cf. John 3:36.
[68] Cf. Mark 3:5.
[69] Eph. 4:26.

sharp-edged sword of anger to fight its battles — that is, to assault and drive off every approach of evil. Without anger, hatred could but smolder in the heart. It needs an instrument of defense and attack, and this was given it by God a power for good that does not hurt the man who uses it aright, but makes him strong and keeps him safe.

But man, alas, can turn away from God and live for himself, or for the things of earth, and in so doing, he changes the center around which the orbit of his life was meant to move, from God to self. He becomes self-centered. But in turning from God, he loses none of the powers of his nature. He finds himself, therefore, possessed of manifold gifts and endowments, all of which were meant to aid him in that moral and spiritual life that leads to God as its end.

These gifts he now uses for himself. Finding in his hand the sword of anger, he seizes it and fights with it his own battles, not the great moral battles for which alone it was intended. He draws it and strikes at everything that hinders him in the pursuit of his own ends, everything that touches his self-love. He uses it for purposes the very reverse of those for which God gave it to him. He can use it to oppose good and to establish evil. Yes, a wild mob with flashing swords of anger, drawn in reckless madness around the cross, striking and wounding the all-holy Son of God, crying, "This is the Heir; come, let us kill Him that the inheritance may be ours":[70] this was indeed the most supreme and most dramatic moment in which men used against God the weapon He had put into their hands to fight His battles.

[70] Cf. Matt. 21:38.

The weapon of anger — let us never forget — is good, God-given, although it may be drawn in a most unworthy cause. It is not the anger that is bad; it is the ill use to which it is put.

The peevish ill temper of a vain woman is essentially the same thing as the splendid moral indignation of the saint. One is used as God meant it to be used; the other is abused for man's unworthy purposes. In one case, the use of it strengthens the steady arm that wields it, and it loses none of its sharpness and luster in the use. In the other case, every blow weakens the hand that strikes, and the weapon itself, with hacked edge and broken blade, forfeits its strength and its glory. There is nothing more noble than the moral indignation of a good man against what is hateful to God. Is there anything more humiliating than the wild and reckless blows of a proud and selfish man, dealt by the blunted and dishonored sword of his misused temper?

∞

Use anger rightly

It will be seen from what has just been said that if we would control our anger so as to prevent its being a source of suffering to others and of injury to ourselves, we shall never really succeed merely by the effort to check it, however faithfully we may try. Still more hopeless would be the effort to destroy it altogether. We could not destroy it even if we wished to, and if we did, we would inflict an irreparable injury upon our character. We need it as an essential part of our moral equipment. It is to be controlled, rather than killed — to be sanctified to the service of God.

We must strive to check it and control it, no doubt, but if we are ever to succeed, we must do more than that. We must strive to conquer that which is the cause of its abuse, and that, as we have seen, is the reign of self in the soul — the living for self instead of for God. As we choose God as the end of our life, more and more steadily every part of our nature will fall into place and work for the development of the soul as His creature and in His service.

The battle with our anger must be both direct and indirect: direct, to check and restrain it when it arises, like a man who has gotten into the habit of putting his hand to his sword on every occasion on which he is vexed; indirect, by the constant effort to dethrone self and set God in its place. Only as this is effected can any victory over temper be lasting or a victory that "does not destroy but fulfills."[71] Only so can we feel sure that we do not lose any of the fire and force of our nature with which God has endowed it.

A perfect victory over anger does not make the man who gained it colorless, tame, or effeminate, any more than it injures a piece of machinery to put back into its place some part that had got out of gear and, by its displacement and undue prominence, hindered the work of the machine. Saul of Tarsus, the hot-headed, intolerant persecutor, lost none of his fire and energy when he became the "slave of Jesus Christ."[72] St. John, the Apostle of Love, was the "Son of Thunder"[73] to the very end.

[71] Cf. Matt. 5:17.
[72] Cf. Rom. 1:1.
[73] Cf. Mark 3:17.

It is, therefore, no easy task. The man who is the slave of anger has allowed that hatred which was originally but the hatred of evil — which is but the other side of love to God — to break away from this love and to exist apart and to act independently. It has no longer anything to do with the love of God. It has passed over to the side of self. Even when it does rise up in anger against evil, it becomes largely a personal feeling of bitterness and irritation. Such hatred has lost its savor, and it is of such that the apostle speaks: "The anger of man worketh not the justice of God."[74] It is not, so to speak, the sharp edge of love; it is rather its enemy. The love of God begets a holy and ennobling hatred of evil; but no hatred, not even such hatred of sin, will ever beget the love of God.

Therefore, to win anger back to be the instrument of the soul's proper warfare, the heart must return to its true home and shelter in God. Loving God, the soul will love all in and for God, and will hate only what God hates, and will draw the sword of anger, sharpened and polished once more by faithful discipline, in the sacred warfare of justice and truth.

∞

Govern even your love

And if anger and hatred are the cause of suffering, love is the unfailing source of happiness. However ungainly and uninteresting a person may be in other ways, love can transform him; however humble and ungifted he is, love endows him with an irresistible power. A man may resist argument or force and feel the stronger for it, but no one ever felt stronger for

[74] James 1:20.

resisting pure love. One who can be conquered by no other power can be conquered by this, and the vanquished is not humbled by his defeat, nor the victor elated by his victory. It is the one thing that binds more closely the conquered and the conqueror.

For love was made to win, and all things were made to yield to it. It is the bond that holds the hosts of Heaven together and binds them to the throne of God; and wherever on earth there is lasting union, love has made it. It can never rest short of possession, and, to gain possession, it will break through every barrier. It was love that brought God down from Heaven so that He might unite Himself to man and lift him up, and this same divine frenzy, when once it has entered the human heart, will not rest until it attains to the possession of God Himself and sits with Christ in heavenly places. What strength it has given to the weak, what courage to the most timid, enabling them "to bear all things, endure all things, hope all things, believe all things,"[75] that they may find rest in God.

This indeed is what love was given us for, to raise us into union with the Infinite, to give us power to conquer the world.

But if we lose sight of God and live for some earthly end, we do not lose this mighty force. We hold it as an integral part of our nature, and we are free to use it as we please. No doubt it loses much of its power and exhausts and wears out the nature that misuses it, but still, even at its weakest, it is great. By it we rise or fall and bind ourselves to God or to earth. It quickens and stimulates every faculty to fight for the possession of that which it desires.

[75] Cf. 1 Cor. 13:7.

Love in the hands of an unprincipled and irresponsible man becomes, therefore, a most dangerous weapon, and if anger and hatred have their victims, so has love. A power that can conquer the world in the hands of a man who has the instincts of a savage is a terrible power. Therefore, to bring happiness to its possessor and to the world it must be disciplined; without discipline, the stronger it is, the fiercer it is.

But, you say, love does not go or come at my bidding; it acts spontaneously. I cannot help loving. Yet God lays His commands even upon our hearts: "Thou shalt love the Lord thy God with thy whole heart."[76] He would not bid us do what is impossible. To bid us love Him is not only to assure us that we can, but also to forbid the love of all that would take us from Him. It is the "first and chief of all the commandments."[77]

Love is not merely a blind passion. It must be controlled by reason. "Love has eyes," and the eye of the heart is the reason.

But it is in its first movements that the outgoing of the heart must be controlled. Later on, it may be impossible. There is a moment in the growth of any undue or unlawful affection when, with comparatively little effort, it could be checked, when conscience and reason give their warning, and if the will exerts itself, all will be well. If such warnings are neglected, the heart quickly breaks away from all control and becomes the most violent of the passions. It is by the yielding in things small and insignificant in themselves, each of which could have been easily resisted, that love becomes an unruly passion

[76] Matt. 22:37.
[77] Cf. Matt. 22:38.

and a source of suffering and misery to its victim and to the world.

On the other hand, it is by small things, often, that the love we owe to others is gradually killed. You may allow your mind to dwell upon the veriest trifles — some little mannerism, some natural defect, the tone of the voice — in a person with a lovable and generous nature, until all the affection you once had and which you owe as a duty is destroyed.

But as it is with anger, so it is with love. Insofar as the soul deflects from God as its true end, so far will it find these great powers that God gave it for edification become a source of destruction. No one can keep his heart in order except by turning it first to God. The power in it is too strong merely to be restrained. It needs an outlet, and the outlet is the infinite being of God. To try to rule our heart in the lesser things of life while its whole current is misdirected is folly. If the river breaks from its channel, and does not hear and obey the call of the ocean, its strength becomes a source of danger. And if the heart is not turned to God, everything that makes it a power for good can make it a power for evil — the intensity of its affection, its loyalty, its fidelity; all these remain to be expended on unworthy or unlawful objects.

Therefore, the affections can be really disciplined only as the current of the soul streams Godward. It is not merely with this or that sin, by excess or defect of love, that we have to deal. To try to love a little more or a little less in such cases would be a vain task. We must look deeper. Only as we try to love God aright can we love man aright. Only by turning our hearts steadily toward God shall we be able to set its movements right toward man.

∞

Let the Commandments help
you govern your love

Now, one great school of the affections is the moral law: the Ten Commandments. Our Lord interprets the whole law as teaching the love of God and the love of man. You will notice the order: not first the love of man, but first the love of God. "This is the first and great commandment: 'Thou shalt love the Lord thy God with thy whole heart, thy whole mind, thy whole soul, and thy whole strength.' The second is like unto it [and necessarily flows from it]: 'Thou shalt love thy neighbor as thyself.' "[78]

It is by placing ourselves under certain laws of commandment and prohibition that the heart becomes trained to turn toward its true end. These commandments say nothing directly about love. But they forbid that which destroys it and direct certain practices that tend to develop it aright. Love is there. Like a stream, it is ever flowing; it needs to be directed into its proper channel, and the soul needs to be warned against that which destroys it.

Take, then, the first four commandments, which teach us our duty to God. Obey these, and the love of God will deepen in your heart; violate them, and your heart will turn away from God. You must allow no rival to God in your heart: "Thou shalt have no other god before me."[79] You must give the worship of your heart to God, you must learn to reverence His holy name, and you must dedicate certain times to His service.

[78] Cf. Matt. 22:37-39.
[79] Cf. Exod. 20:3.

Violate one or all of these, and your love of God will fail or die; obey them, and the stream of your affections will flow in its true channel — Godward.

How true to experience it is that the loss of all love of God can be traced to the breach of one or more of these commandments. Some idol is set up in the heart and becomes His rival. The worship of His holy name is neglected. The spirit of lowly reverence is lost. The times that should be devoted to His service are neglected, and God has ceased to be loved.

And it is only by the observance of the first and greatest commandment that we can keep the second. The more we love God, the more we shall love man; the less we love God, the less we shall, in the true sense of the word, love man. Our love will become capricious, fitful, and unreliable — not charity, but passion.

If you feel that your love for your fellowmen is dying out in the fumes of selfishness, there is but one way to revive it: strive for, pray for, the love of God. As the heart turns toward its source, it will be quickened and expanded. There is no true, no lasting spirit of charity apart from the practice of religion.

Therefore, we cannot keep those commandments which teach us our duty to men unless we are keeping those which teach us our duty to God. These last educate and discipline our affections toward one another. They begin with the first duty of children to their parents and regulate and control the outgoings of the heart toward others, forbidding hate, lust, selfishness, insincerity, and covetousness; controlling unlawful desires, checking passion in its beginning, and thus keeping the heart pure and its currents flowing in their proper channels.

If you find that you fail in charity, ask yourself whether, by loving in a wrong way or by failing to love as you ought, by loving too much or loving too little, there is any one of the Ten Commandments you are deliberately breaking. Are you yielding to anger or sensuality, or selfishness, or unkindness in speech, or discontent, or envy and jealousy? All these, or any of them, injure or wholly destroy that spirit of charity which is the love of God manifesting itself in the human heart toward its fellow creatures.

Love must be thus trained and disciplined, and the "law is the schoolmaster." Obey the law, place yourself under its commands and restraints, and your love will cease to be passion, and, guided by reason, it will be a source of blessing to you and to the world.

Chapter Seven

∞

Govern your body

∞

The revelation God has given to His Church is at once stimulating and disappointing. It is stimulating inasmuch as it deals
with matters so great and of such vast interest to mankind and
that affect us so intimately. It is disappointing in that it fails to
answer so many questions we long to have answered.

It confines itself chiefly to two points: the meaning and
reason of man's present mysterious state and the method of his
restoration. All else is subsidiary to this: the Fall and the
Restoration of man. The revelation is made to man and for
man, and always for practical, not speculative, ends. It does
not satisfy our curiosity, however reverent and natural that
curiosity may be, but confines itself to the purpose it has in
hand.

It is remarkable that while the mystery of man's being has
always been the subject of study and speculation, fascinating
and perplexing beyond all others, the greatest minds of antiq-
uity seem never to have come anywhere near the simple solu-
tion that revelation gives: that man is created in the image of
God, and fallen. He is in the image of God, and is therefore
ever haunted by great ideals; ever seeking after God and striving to be Godlike. He is fallen, and the jar of the Fall has

dislocated his whole being and robbed him of that supernatural gift which preserved the order and harmony of his nature and kept the body under the control of the spirit.

Wherever we turn throughout history, we know that men were feeling that struggle of the flesh with the spirit of which we are ourselves so conscious. However far back we look, however strange the life men lived, one thing enables us to bridge the ages and to enter into sympathy with them. Whatever their interests and aims, and however different from ours, these men and women were like us in this at least: they knew and felt what we feel. Beneath the surface, there was the same struggle, issuing as it does today in the life of each individual, in the victory of the spirit over the flesh or of the flesh over the spirit.

Yet, as to the cause of this struggle, their speculations resulted mainly in the conclusion that matter was evil and the soul divine, and that these must struggle until the soul was emancipated and set free from contact with matter.

Now, in the Gospel we find two classes of sayings about the body: one of warning, the other speaking of its honor and dignity.

We read such words of St. Paul as these: "Mortify the members of your body, which are upon the earth";[80] "If you live according to the flesh you shall die, but if by the Spirit you mortify the deeds of the flesh you shall live";[81] and again, "He that soweth in his flesh shall of the flesh reap corruption, but he that soweth in the spirit shall of the spirit reap life

---

[80] Cf. Col. 3:5.
[81] Cf. Rom. 8:13.

ever-lasting."[82] The flesh is set against the spirit in such passages as being the source of danger, corruption, and death. To live after the flesh is to die; to mortify the flesh is to live.

In contrast to these passages we read such words as: "Your members are the temple of the Holy Spirit";[83] "The body is not for fornication, but for the Lord, and the Lord for the body";[84] "Shall I take the members of Christ and make them members of a harlot?"[85] And in the most solemn moments of our communion with God, when we try to forget the flesh and to rise on the wings of the spirit, it is on the Body of our Lord that we feed our souls.

We are conscious of something corresponding with both these classes of sayings in our own experience.

There are moments when it seems to us as if the source of all the evil were in the flesh. We feel "the corruptible flesh weighing down the incorruptible spirit." We feel the tides of passion and materialism that take their rise in the flesh, wash over and swamp the spirit until, for the moment, the animal nature appears to be wholly triumphant. And we know how true St. Paul's words are: "If you live according to the flesh, you shall die."

But again, there are times when the body itself seems lifted up and partakes of and adds to the joys of the spirit. Wave after wave of spiritual joy sweeps through the open channels of the flesh and fills it with a new and intoxicating joy, before which

[82] Cf. Gal. 6:8.
[83] Cf. 1 Cor. 6:19.
[84] 1 Cor. 6:13.
[85] Cf. 1 Cor. 6:15.

the pleasures of the flesh seem poor and sickly. At such moments we are dimly aware of the possibility of the body, after a long process of training and discipline, being uplifted and spiritualized and entering into a closer, more intimate union with the life of the soul, where the lust of the flesh against the spirit and the spirit against the flesh would be at an end. Then we know that the flesh is not evil, nor the source of all evil in our life.

> Let us not always say, "Spite of the flesh today
> I strove, made head and gained ground on the whole."
> As the bird wings and sings, let us say, "All good things
> Are ours, nor soul helps flesh more now
>   than flesh helps soul."[86]

Yet such moments of spiritual exaltation are rare and often have to be paid for by a reaction in which the flesh renews with greater violence its assaults upon the spirit. They hold out to us no certain prospect of such a happy union here on earth as that of which the poet speaks wherein "nor soul helps flesh more now than flesh helps soul." On the contrary, although they may be the earnest of a perfect union to come — like the Transfiguration of our Lord — a moment of prophetic vision of what shall be hereafter, they warn us that the warfare has by no means ended, that there is need of renewed vigilance and self-discipline.

But apart from such rare moments of exaltation, which support and are themselves illuminated by the teachings of revelation, men might well ask if this age-long conflict between

---

[86] Browning, "Rabbi Ben Ezra."

flesh and spirit is never to come to an end — if there is no remedy to heal this strange discord in the highest of God's creatures upon earth.

The witness of each individual is that it is persistent and unceasing from the dawn of consciousness until it is lost in death; that no one can remember its beginning, and, so far as experience goes, it has no end on earth; that we do not escape from it either by yielding to the flesh or by living for the spirit. The saint bears upon his face the marks of this ceaseless struggle; the most sensual bears those traces of the protests of the baffled spirit that show that man is not a mere animal. No one has yet reached that spiritual height where he could relax his watchfulness and cease to struggle. There are stories told of those who, after years of self-discipline and mortification, grew careless and relaxed their vigilance and fell.

However far we look back into the past, this dualism is seen wherever man is found, and there is no sign or token of its ceasing, nor of the conflict between flesh and spirit becoming less acute. There is no living member of the human race who can say he has found the remedy and made a truce. We, who are the children of a later age and have heard the prophets of our own day prophesy great things and declare the wonders that are to be wrought by science and education and a deeper knowledge of the laws of life, know full well that however great the enrichment of life in material things, and however wide the spread of knowledge, not the smallest step has been taken toward setting man at one with himself.

We cannot suppose that the God of order and unity created man in this state of disorder, an exception to all His other works. Yet we find no human record of its beginning; we find no hope, no hint, of any prospect of its ending. What, then, is to be the end of it?

∞

Do not try to crush the spirit or the body
One of two things alone seems possible if this strife is not to be eternal.

Some have lived as though they would trample upon and conquer the spirit, until the last spark of its life is drowned, as the unchained passions of the flesh burst forth like the loosened waters and swamp it, and unity is purchased at the price of that which raises man above the beasts. There have indeed been times in the past when it has almost seemed as if it would be so. There are men in our own time who seem to have well-nigh succeeded in beating out the man and beating in the beast. But however low they may have sunk, however strong the animal nature and weak the spiritual, it still lives on if only to rebuke and condemn — "a spark disturbs this clod, a sting that bids nor sit nor stand, but go." Man cannot destroy it and be happy as a beast. When he has sunk to the lowest depths, "and fain would fill his belly with the husks that the swine did eat,"[87] he begins to dream about his Father's home and the possibility of arising from his degradation. He has tried hard enough and long enough to destroy the dualism that torments him by slaying his spiritual nature — men try it still — but it is impossible, for it is his very self.

Others have sought to bring the inner strife to an end by the destruction of the flesh. They have looked upon the flesh

[87] Luke 15:16.

as a snare in which man, who is a spiritual being, has become entangled. If he would trample upon it, despise it, starve it to death, and try to live as much as possible as if he had no body, the spirit would gain strength as the coils of the flesh were loosened, and at last the soul would cast it aside forever in death like a dishonored and threadbare garment and live henceforth as a pure spirit.

But against such a theory we may notice two things. First, the asceticism that seeks such a deliverance itself bears witness to its untruth. It leaves upon the soul that so treats the body the marks of its revenge. The body refuses to be so sacrificed without leaving the deep impress of its protest in the moral injuries it inflicts upon the soul. We have but to look at the effects of heathen asceticism to feel that it is a violation of nature. The soul does not rise or grow strong; it becomes dreamy and unreal. Between such practice and that of Christian asceticism there is as much difference as there is between life and death.

On the other hand, the body will often revolt against being treated with unreasonable severity, still more against any effort to ignore it, and will assault the soul with those very temptations from which it sought to escape. If we try to ignore it, it will become more insistent in its demands. If we treat it too harshly, it will make us feel its power.

∞

The Fall destroyed the union of soul and body
We cannot end this inner conflict, therefore, by the killing off of either one or the other; each refuses to be slain, and the effort only increases our anguish.

What, then — is this discord to go on forever? And is man to be content to struggle on in darkness with no light as to its origin or end?

Age after age went by; the struggle waxed fiercer and fiercer; times were when the flesh seemed wholly victorious and the spirit dethroned and dishonored; men questioned one another as to what was to be the end. But no complete answer was given until Christ came. He came and laid open the secret not only of the future but of the past.

His answer to man was this. This dualism that rends and tortures you is not of God's making, but your own. It had a beginning, and it will have an end. It is the penalty of that act of disobedience whereby Adam sacrificed the supernatural union with God that held the body subject to the soul. The soul unaided is not able to keep the whole nature in harmonious order.

Man's nature was never intended to be complete in itself; it was created so that it could fulfill itself and its destiny only by union with God. That union was lost by sin. Then began the conflict, "the flesh lusting against the spirit and the spirit against the flesh." But the body, however rebellious, is an integral part of man's nature. He must be saved body and soul, or he cannot be saved at all. Men must pay the penalty of the Fall — that inner conflict which ends only in the separation of soul and body in death.

But the body shall rise again, and the risen and glorified body shall live in perfect union with the soul. Then "they shall no more hunger nor thirst, neither shall the sun fall upon them, nor any heat. For the Lamb which is in the midst of the throne shall rule them and shall lead them into the fountains of the waters of life . . . and wipe away all tears from their eyes."[88]

The answer, then, of Christian revelation to man's perplexity lies in disclosing the past and the future, the Fall and the resurrection.

Between these is the dispensation of Christ, wherein He bestows upon man the supernatural gift of grace by which once more he is restored to union with God. This gift does not indeed establish that inner harmony which was forfeited once and for all by the Fall. But it bestows upon man a power by which he can gain control over the flesh to discipline and train its rebellions and teach it to take its place of subordination as the soul's servant and not its master, and thus prepare it for the resurrection, when once more, body and soul will meet and live forever in that perfect union which knows no strife or discord.

The doctrine of the resurrection thus protects the doctrine of the Fall. It impresses upon us the fact that the body is an integral part of our nature, that the conflict between flesh and spirit that was caused by the Fall ends when its penalty has been paid, and man is restored once more in the completeness of his nature.

Give up the doctrine of the Resurrection, and the doctrine of the Fall goes with it, and, with that, the doctrine of the Incarnation: "If there be no resurrection . . . then is not Christ risen again, and if Christ be not risen again, then . . . your faith is also vain."[89]

[88] Rev. 7:16-17.
[89] 1 Cor. 15:13-14.

Thus, in His life on earth, our Lord refused to deal with man merely as a spiritual being. In all His actions, in every work of healing, what was the instrument with which He healed? It was His body. His touch restored the dead to life. The moisture from His lips gave light to the sightless eyes. His fingers pierced the closed ears of the deaf and opened them to hearing. The very touch of His garments, steeped in the power that flowed forth from Him, healed the woman bowed down with disease. In all His dealings with man, He dealt with him as a composite being and taught him to reverence the flesh.

In that kingdom which He came on earth to found — the Catholic Church — it is the same. Every great spiritual gift that is given to cement man's union with Christ is bestowed upon him through material channels.

Thus would our Lord impress upon His followers that the body is an integral part of man's nature, to be neither indulged nor ill-treated, but by the help of His grace, and by the practice of constant discipline, to be brought back to that position of dignity and true liberty as cooperator with the soul in the service of God, which it held before the Fall.

And it is in the hope of the resurrection that this is to be done.

In its essence and in its motive, Christian asceticism is absolutely different from that of the heathens. Heathen asceticism would get rid of the body as an enemy to be hated; Christian asceticism would train it for its glorious life in Heaven. The heathen ascetic has ever before him the thought of death; the Christian, the thought of the resurrection. For whatever changes will have passed upon the body in the resurrection, the organic unity between the risen and mortal flesh will be preserved: "In my flesh I shall see God."[90]

∞

Your character affects your body

The deeds that the body does upon earth, the habits it forms, and the life it lives must as surely affect its future as they affect the future of the soul. Character is stamped upon the whole bodily frame; the way a man walks or sits or stands all help to show something of his character. We are told that every thought is registered in the molecular changes that it effects in the brain.

And certainly the face is the mirror in which the soul is reflected, upon which it stamps with ever-deepening lines its thoughts, its passions, and its ambitions. The difference between the face of a child and the face of a man is the same as that between a white sheet of paper and one covered with writing, or between a new garment and one that has been long worn.

It has been said by a well-known and learned psychologist, "I believe that we are subject to the law of habit in consequence of the fact that we have bodies. The plasticity of the living matter of our nervous system, in short, is the reason why we do a thing with difficulty the first time, but soon do it more and more easily, and finally, with sufficient practice, do it semi-mechanically, or with hardly any consciousness at all. Our nervous systems have *grown* to the way in which they have been exercised, just as a sheet of paper or a coat once

[90] Cf. Job 19:26.

creased or folded tends to fall forever afterward into the same identical folds."[91]

Had we but eyes to see, we might take scalpel and micro-scope and read in the bodily frame the moral history of the life of the soul that was its tenant. Indeed, many a characteristic is stamped so clearly that none can fail to see it. Many we fain would hide but cannot; the telltale flesh has, so to speak, materialized the thoughts of the mind, given them form and shape, and revealed them to the world.

As the body lies still and silent in death, its mystery and its pathos is that it has been the instrument and cooperator, and remains the material record of the soul's life. No thought ever passed through the mind for one brief moment without the body taking its part and writing the record. Was ever history written with such unerring accuracy as is written the history of the soul in the body it inhabits?

∞

Your self-discipline will affect
your resurrected body

And this body must rise again. Whatever changes it may have to undergo, it is the same body, the partner of the soul here on earth, the material crystallization of the life of the immaterial soul; the servant that often gained the mastery and entangled the body in its meshes and seduced it to sin. The body must rise again, bearing upon it for good or evil the traces of its earthly life.

---

[91] William James, *Talks to Teachers on Psychology* (New York: Henry Holt and Company, c. 1899).

If, then, we are able to form any conception of the condition of the risen body, it will help us and guide us in the practice of self-discipline. The object of all such discipline is to subdue the flesh and bring it into a state of obedience, and thus prepare it for its life in the resurrection.

Can we, then, form any idea of the glorified body? For if we can, we shall know better what our aim is, and we shall find in it the principles that are to govern us in the practice of the discipline of our mortal bodies. We shall have a model by which to guide ourselves, and we shall not be overbold if we expect to find here on earth some dim foreshadowings of what that life is to be beyond the grave.

Now, St. Paul gives us four characteristics of the glorified body: "It is sown in corruption, it shall rise in incorruption. It is sown in dishonor, it shall rise in glory. It is sown in weakness, it shall rise in power. It is sown a natural body, it shall rise a spiritual body."[92]

We cannot indeed expect to find any tokens of the incorruption, or the glory, or the power, or the spirituality of the risen body while we are here on earth, however faithful and strict we may be in the practice of self-discipline. But I think we can and may expect to experience within ourselves that from which such results will follow — to feel those spiritual movements within the soul and that taming of the body which is preparatory to it, as the first movements of the spring are preparatory to the full glory of the summer.

Let us consider these four characteristics that St. Paul gives us and see how we can use them as principles of self-discipline

[92] 1 Cor. 15:42-44.

by which the body may be prepared for their full enjoyment hereafter.

∞

Deny your body whatever weakens
your soul's union with God

"It is sown in corruption, it shall rise in incorruption." The body here on earth is ever prone to suffering and decay, ever face-to-face with death. The fuel of life is constantly consumed and needs to be supplied afresh. We can neither act nor think except by the expenditure of energy that, if it cannot be renewed, is soon exhausted. But in the resurrection, all pain and suffering and decay will have passed away forever. "There shall be no more sorrow nor suffering, for the former things are passed away."[93]

The shadow of death no longer lies across the pathway; it lies behind. The soul can look back and see the gate of death thrown open, the secrets of the grave laid bare, and its mystery exposed. Its terrors lie behind. It looks forward and sees the open plains of endless life bathed in unclouded light.

When last the soul and body were united, the agony of death was upon it; every nerve was on the rack as they grappled in their final struggle. Now they have met and are united once more, and through the veins there surges the currents of a life so strong that the memories of the keenest moments of youth seem like the splutterings of a dying candle compared with it. Time has no meaning, and work no power of wearying. There streams through every channel of the flesh a torrent of

[93] Cf. Rev. 21:4.

inexhaustible energy that never flags. Ages go by, and the body is untouched by time in the exhilaration of perennial youth. The energy of the divine life breathes from its nostrils, shines upon its brow, and radiates from its presence.

How could suffering or death approach such a being who fills the whole air with its pulsing life? And this is the body that toiled and suffered on earth, seeking to husband its failing strength and vitality so that it might live out the threescore years and ten of its earthly pilgrimage.[94]

Where does the body get this wonderful life? Never in the most exuberant days of its youth did it have anything like it. From where, then, has it received it? The body has not *within itself* the gift of immortality. Yet it knows that, with such a life flowing in its veins, suffering and death are impossible. How, then, has the frail and suffering flesh been so transformed, and where does that torrent of life that transforms it come from?

Its source is in the soul, not in the body; it flows out upon the body from the soul. The soul is so strong, the vigor of its life so great, that everything gives way before it as it goes coursing through the veins and flooding the body with its energy. As the darkness flies from the face of the morning sun, so do suffering and death fly before this mighty stream of life.

But where does the soul get this power? It received it here on earth. Its first germs were imparted to it at the baptismal font. "This is the testimony that God hath given to us: eternal life. And this life is in His Son. He that hath the Son hath life,

---

[94] Cf. Ps. 89:10 (RSV = Ps. 90:10).

and he that hath not the Son hath not life."[95] And again, "I am come that they may have life, and that they may have it more abundantly."[96]

This more abundant life given in Baptism is nourished by the sacraments and developed by the struggle with sin. It springs from union with Him who is the Fountain and Source of eternal life. That life now flowing with such energy had to be cultivated and developed amid all the difficulties of earth. Often it was so weak and nature so strong that its pulses were scarcely felt beating, but every struggle strengthened it; every sacrament increased its power. And now, when the soul's probation is ended and every difficulty is overcome and its union with Christ is perfected, behold, the life that is in it pours out upon the flesh, transforming it and making it partaker of its joys.

To gain this glorious gift for the body, the soul, when on earth, had to carry on a constant warfare with it — to discipline it, to refuse its demands, and to check its encroachments. Often it had to be stern with the body, sometimes perhaps to inflict suffering upon it in order to tame it. But it is with no Manichaean idea that the body is inherently evil; no, it is to gain for it this glorious bridal gift of immortality with which to endow it on the morning of the resurrection.

Let this, then, be the first principle in the practice of self-discipline: to refuse to the body all that can weaken or delay the soul's union with our Lord. Let that be ever the first and ruling aim in life, and when the body is insistent in its demands

[95] 1 John 5:11-12.
[96] John 10:10.

for what might mar that union, it is good to remember that by refusing it indulgence, we are gaining for it a better indulgence: immunity from suffering for all eternity. Every such act of self-discipline is inspired by the highest reason and looks through the moment's suffering to the gain that it secures for eternity.

∞

Cultivate the fire of holiness
in your soul

"It is sown in dishonor, it shall rise in glory." The last that is seen of the body on earth is as it passes beneath the shadow of death and is robbed of every ornament of beauty with which life endowed it. When next that same body is seen, it is glorified; it shines with a light that transforms it. "Then shall the just shine."[97] Here we clothe ourselves with garments that are to remind us of our fallen state; there the body needs no garments: "It is decked with light as with a garment."[98] The pallor and dishonor of death have passed from it as night passes before the coming day.

But from where does the body have this brightness? It receives it from the soul. The body has become, as it were, a lantern through which the radiant soul shines.

And the soul? When was it set on fire by this divine light that radiates forth from it and does not consume it? The first spark of that fire was kindled within it on earth and had to be tended and guarded through all earth's storms and troubles. "I

---

[97] Matt. 13:43.
[98] Cf. Ps. 103:2 (RSV = Ps. 104:2).

am come," said our Lord, "to send fire upon the earth."[99] It is
the gift of holiness, the presence in the soul of that Spirit who
came down upon the Apostles at Pentecost in the form of fiery
tongues.[100]

That fire is first kindled in Baptism, and the work of life is
to fan it into a brighter and ever brighter flame. The fire must
be within, shining outward from within. "He was a burning and
a shining light"[101] — first burning and then shining. There are
many who have a wonderful power of catching and reflecting
the light of another as it shines upon them from without; such
light leaves the person who reflects it in darkness when it is
withdrawn. It is not merely the reflection of another's influence that will adorn both body and soul with light eternally.

We must therefore have the fire of personal holiness burning within us and shining forth from us, however dimly here, if
hereafter we are to shine as stars in the heavens. "You," says
our Lord, "are the light of the world"; and again, "Let your
light shine."[102] The foolish virgins in the hour of death awakened to find their lamps going out and the door of the heavenly kingdom closed against them, while the wise trimmed
their lamps and went forth to meet the Bridegroom.[103]

The work of life, then, is to tend the divine fire of holiness
that has been kindled within against every breath that may
endanger it; and every holy deed and thought helps to feed

[99] Cf. Luke 12:49.
[100] Acts 2:3.
[101] John 5:35.
[102] Matt. 5:14, 16.
[103] Matt. 25:1-12.

and fan the flame. In proportion to the brightness of the fire that burns within when the soul goes forth to meet its Judge will be the glory with which it will clothe the body in the morning of the resurrection. "One is the glory of the sun, another the glory of the moon, and another the glory of the stars; for star differeth from star in glory. So also is the resurrection of the dead."[104] And the glory with which these heavenly constellations shine is kindled here on earth.

But there is another fire that may burn within us, before whose lurid flames the divine light grows pale and dim and at last dies out: the fire that at first, as the faintest spark, burns in the flesh and grows with a fearful rapidity, demanding ever more and more fuel, until all that is noblest in the soul is sacrificed to feed its all-consuming flames, and the heavenly flame dies exhausted and untended.

Therefore, we have constantly to make our choice. We cannot keep both these fires alight within us; we must starve one so that we may feed the other. In feeding the divine fire in the soul, the fire within the flesh must die for lack of food. We may try to trample upon it and extinguish it; we may make violent and exhausting efforts, only to find that it has flamed out more furiously. We shall never put it out by such methods. There is only one safe and certain way. Use all your efforts in feeding the fire of the soul; sacrifice to it all that the flesh could feed upon, and that deadly fire will die for lack of nourishment. "Walk in the spirit, and you shall not fulfill the lusts of the flesh."[105] He who gives all his thoughts and efforts to tending

[104] 1 Cor. 15:41-42.
[105] Gal. 5:16.

the fire from Heaven will in time find that the earthly fire has exhausted itself.

This is the only safe way to meet the demands of the flesh when they rise up against the spirit — indirectly rather than directly; positively rather than negatively. As the spirit grows stronger, the flesh grows weaker. No man ever succeeded in merely chaining his passions. The one remedy is to turn to God, to live closer to Him, to deny the body by turning all our interests and all our energies to the cultivation of the spirit. As the disorder of nature is thus overcome, the passions, purified and disciplined, sink into their proper place.

∞

Submit your flesh to your spirit

"It is sown in weakness, it shall rise in power." When last the body was seen, it was in the weakness of fast-approaching dissolution. It could not minister to its own wants. Exhaustion paralyzed every member. With faltering and feeble steps, the feet had taken their last journey and refused to bear the body any farther. The hand could not lift the food to the lips, the weary eyes could look no longer on the sights of earth, and the soul imprisoned in the worn-out frame of the body could no longer express itself. As the quick breath comes from the heaving chest and burning lips, and the sweat stands thick upon the brows, and the faltering lips refuse to frame the broken and inarticulate words, the dying body presents a picture of the utmost weariness and exhaustion. The journey of life leaves it cast at the gate of the grave too weak, too utterly worn out, to take one step farther. Verily it is "sown in weakness."

That is the last that is seen of the body before the thread of life is broken and the soul slips forth in solitude.

And when next it is seen, it is as a giant refreshed with wine. It wakens from the sleep of death to find itself renewed, invigorated, energized, with a power that is inexhaustible and unwearied. On earth, the body has to drag itself after the mind by slow and weary movements, but now the body is borne along on the strong wings of the soul; it flashes with the swiftness of thought from place to place. The movements of the whole man are in perfect union; no longer does the corruptible flesh weigh down the incorruptible spirit, but the imponderable flesh, penetrated with the energy of the spirit, keeps step with it in its glorious movements.

From where, then, has it received this gift? It falls to sleep in death in the utmost exhaustion. It wakens to the life of the resurrection renewed with an energy that transforms it. Again we answer: this gift is not inherent in the body; it is imparted to it from the soul. But from where did the soul receive it? It showed no such power during its earthly life; on the contrary, often the vigor of the soul's life is gained at the expense of the weakening of the body.

Yet, if no such power was manifested in the soul here on earth, there surely were anticipations of it. There were manifestations of a divine energy that nothing could repress or destroy, an indomitable spirit that would lash the body on, however weary or ailing, and force it to obey.

This energy was awakened by no hope of earthly reward and was often alien to the natural man. It is not of earth but of Heaven. It is imparted to the soul through its union with our Lord by the gift of divine grace.

It was of this gift our Lord spoke when He said, "The zeal of Thy house hath eaten me up."[106] It was of this that His great servant spoke when he cried, "This one thing I do: forgetting the things that are behind . . . I press toward the mark, to the prize of the supernal vocation of God in Christ Jesus."[107] This indomitable power St. Paul manifested through his life, bearing along his feeble body in the arms of his triumphant soul: "in stripes, in prisons, in seditions, in labors, in watchings, in fastings."[108] Nothing could hold back that spirit set on fire from above, and the poor, exhausted body must obey and follow as he drags it in his tempestuous zeal from east to west, from one end of Europe to the other.

Each in his measure and degree must manifest some spark of that divine power here on earth if he is to enrich the body with it hereafter. The tired body cries out against the soul's activity. "The spirit is willing, but the flesh is weak."[109] Yet every victory of the spirit over the flesh will gain a richer endowment for the flesh that submits; every surrender to the flesh will be for it an eternal loss. Every hour of prayer, every night of vigil, every day of fasting, every work of charity, and every act of mercy done for the love of God and kindled by the fire of holy zeal, in spite of the protests of the flesh, will strengthen in the spirit that divine energy which will enable it in the morning of the resurrection to endue the body with its strength.

[106] Ps. 68:10 (RSV = Ps. 69:9).
[107] Cf. Phil. 3:13-14.
[108] 2 Cor. 6:5.
[109] Cf. Matt. 26:41.

∞

Avoid indulging your body

"It is sown a natural body, it shall rise a spiritual body." We must not suppose that when St. Paul says, "It shall rise a spiritual body," he means that it shall cease to be a body. Let me repeat it: man is by nature composed of body and soul; he will never be as the angels, pure spirits. "He took not hold of the angels, but of the seed of Abraham He took hold."[110] Human nature after death is not changed into angelic nature. By "a spiritual body," it is not meant that the body has ceased to be a body and that man has undergone so fundamental a change that he has practically ceased to be man.

What, then, does it mean? It means that the body receives some of the attributes of a spirit, that it lives henceforth a spirit's life; it becomes spiritualized.

There is something analogous to this in the natural order. The most solid substances under the action of heat take the form of gas. Although they remain chemically unchanged, their properties are so changed that it is impossible for the untrained eye to recognize them. A heavy mass becomes buoyant, elastic, transparent, and a weight that a strong man could not lift floats as vapor in the air.

Something analogous to this takes place in the risen body. The soul aflame with the fire of God's presence acts upon the body as fire upon solid matter and transforms and spiritualizes it. The heat of the burning soul transmutes it. It is flesh still, as truly as every atom of the steam was once solid ice, but it is spiritualized, transformed, glorified. The intensity of the

---

[110] Cf. Heb. 2:16.

spirit's life radiates through every nerve and fiber, burns out all that is gross and earthly, and lifts it into a perfect partnership with its own glorious life.

This power which works such wonders in the resurrection is bestowed upon the soul here on earth, and if it is to produce its full effects hereafter, it must be developed amid the difficulties of this life. The soul, by the power of divine grace and kindling with the fire of the love of God, must strive as much as may be to spiritualize the body, refining it and purifying it more and more from the coarseness and grossness of its natural state. There are many things short of sin in which the body can be permitted or refused indulgence — all those things by which the light of faith is dimmed and the soul is endangered of losing some of its luster. The stronger the hold the good things of this world have upon the body, the weaker the soul becomes. There is such a thing as living *in* the senses — the delight of the senses in their own enjoyment — what St. Paul calls "walking after the flesh." It is not what is ordinarily meant by *sensuality*; we may live such a life and never even be tempted to sensual sin. But it is the reverse of spiritual. In proportion as we live such a life, the spiritual life becomes weakened and the things of faith lose some of their power.

In the struggle with the body to overcome this tendency — to walk in the spirit, not after the flesh; to deny it pleasures that, although not sinful, have the danger of becoming inordinate — the soul develops that power which, in the resurrection, lifts the body into that union with itself by which it is "raised a spiritual body."

For our encouragement, we are permitted sometimes to see here on earth men and women who have so advanced in the spiritual life that they seem to have come as near this as it is possible in this life. Their bodies seem almost etherealized. They satisfy the body's wants so far as it is necessary to keep it alive, and that is all. They reduce its wants to a minimum, but their life, their joys are chiefly those of the spirit.

Thus, the resurrection becomes the most practical thought in the daily life of the devout Catholic. The vision whose dim outlines are ever before his eyes becomes the model by which he works, and its laws are the principles by which he trains the body for its beatitude, when the dualism of earth will have ceased, and, grasped in the mighty arms of the soul, it will enter into its joy and partake of its glory.

Chapter Eight

∞

Sacrifice the good for what is better

∞

There are two words that echo throughout the teaching of our Lord and His Apostles: *life* and *death*. Different people, according to the difference of temperament and training, take up one or the other of these words as the keynote of their spiritual life.

The gospel of Jesus Christ, say some, "is a gospel of life. It breathes with the vigor of a fresh, energetic life from beginning to end. 'In Him was life, and the life was the light of men.' 'I am come that they may have life, and may have it more abundantly.' 'You will not come unto me that you may have life.' 'I am the Resurrection and the Life. . . . He that believeth in me shall never die.' 'I am the Bread of Life.' 'The law of the Spirit of Life delivered me from the law of sin and of death.'[111] From first to last, it is full of this thought of living rather than dying, of giving forth rather than restraint, of letting yourself go in energetic action rather than holding yourself back in timid self-repression. What we need is not to die but to live and to live more abundantly, to die to sin by living to righteousness, conquering evil by good. If we thought less of

[111] Cf. John 1:4, 10:10, 5:40 (RSV = John 5:39), 11:25-26, 6:35; Rom. 8:2.

ourselves and gave ourselves out more to others, we would get rid of a multitude of faults bred of self-analysis and morbid self-repression."

So these men tell us that the gospel is a gospel of life, and in life, not death, in action rather than in mortification, we are to find the remedy for our needs. As we hear them speak, still more as we watch them live, we feel that they certainly have not the whole of the truth, and part of a truth is often very misleading. There is too much talk about life and living to be healthy, too much of the very self-consciousness that is deprecated, too little taking in. It all seems to be giving out, and a good deal of it a waste of energy. Somehow such people, although they may quote the words of our Lord about living, seem very far from reproducing the calm, strong life that He lived and taught.

There are others who read the teaching of our Lord very differently, who say, "No, His gospel is a gospel of death. Its message of hope and joy is only for those who are ready to give up all and to die for it. 'If any man will come after me, let him deny himself and take up his cross daily and follow me.' 'He that saveth his life shall lose it; he that loseth his life shall find it.' 'Unless the grain of wheat falling into the ground die, it remaineth alone, but if it die, it shall bring forth much fruit.' 'We are buried with Him by Baptism into death.' 'If you live after the flesh you shall die, but if by the Spirit you mortify the deeds of the flesh, you shall live.' 'I die daily,' says St. Paul. 'I bear about in my body the marks of the Lord Jesus.' [112] The

---

[112] Cf. Luke 9:25; Matt. 16:25; John 12:24-25; Col. 2:12; Rom. 8:13; 1 Cor. 15:31; Gal. 6:17.

gospel of Christ is a gospel of death. We must die to everything that is of earth so that we may gain the things of Heaven. We must mortify every earthly passion, every human feeling and desire. The very beauty of this fair earth has its subtle danger. Better turn our backs and close our eyes to it and wait for the beauty of that land that lies beyond."

As we listen to such words and watch the lives of those who teach them, we feel again that they may have part of our Lord's teaching, but certainly they have not the whole. In their lives we feel the chill and rigor of death, but a death that has little cheer or hope and still less love. We must always respect the sincerity and courage of those who are ready to deny themselves and who reduce life's pleasures and comforts to a minimum. But we do not feel inclined to follow them or to believe that they have the true secret of that gospel which sets men's hearts on fire. God has not given us things *merely* that we should give them up, or powers *merely* that we should not use them.

For the fact is, each of these has taken one side of our Lord's teaching and ignored the other.

These two words, *life* and *death*, ring out with equal distinctness and ever-recurrent rhythm, one always following close on the other. Now our Lord seems to be speaking about that life which He came to give, and which He would have us live, and, lo, He is speaking of death. Again, He is speaking of the cross and the tomb, and behold, it is of life He speaks. They are never separated in the teaching of our Lord. Neither stands alone. And it is the part of those who would follow Him to reconcile these two principles in their own practical lives.

No doubt it is easier to take one of them and try to produce that, but it will not be the Christian life. You may die to every-thing that the world has to give; or you may live with the stream of life ever at full flood. But you will not have that ex-quisite grace, that wonderful blending of opposite characteris-tics so free from extremes, so essentially true, that is the marked product of the faithful following of the teaching of Christ.

If Christ's teaching reconciles life and death, which are ever in deadly antagonism, no wonder it brings together and harmonizes in the soul other characteristics that are seemingly irreconcilable.

We must, then, in our practical life constantly bring to-gether these two principles of life and death. Death must ever suggest — if I may say so, bring with it — some new experi-ence of life; and life must always have upon it the shadow of the tomb, or, better still, the light that shines upon it from the other side. Death is not all darkness, nor life all light. The light of life illuminates and warms the pallor of death. The daily dying is robbed of the chill coldness of the tomb, for in the agony of death, the heart seems only to grow warmer and more human. Life is freed from the noise and bluster that so vulgarize it and gains something of the reverence and restraint of the chamber of death.

∞

Do not use mortification
as an end in itself

A life without any mortification quickly runs to seed, and mortification practiced as an end in itself soon degenerates into hardness and cynicism. In every act of dying, we must gaze into the tomb with the Magdalene until we see it transformed by the vision of life and beauty that lies beyond it and shines through it. And in every act of living, there must be just that element of mortification which prevents us from draining life down to the dregs and exhausting its energies in the death of decay, from which there is no door into any life beyond. We all know the weariness and disappointment that follow quickly upon the footsteps of self-indulgence.

We must keep this principle before ourselves constantly in the practice of mortification, if we would get good from it instead of harm. There is no particular advantage in the *mere* act of giving up what we like. The idea of giving up the good things of this life, its pleasures and enjoyments, simply because it is better in itself to be without them, is assuredly a mistaken one. There is not necessarily any spiritual advantage in the mere act of depriving ourselves of anything in itself harmless. The fact of *not* having does not make a man better than the fact of *having*. Many a man suffering from grinding poverty would conceivably have been a better man and a better Christian if he had not been so poor. In itself, it is better, broadly speaking, to have than not to have, to have a full life than an empty life, to have health and friends and the power of enjoyment than not to have them. A man who has everything this world can give him is not *necessarily* a worse man or a less spiritual man than one who has nothing.

Still less can we suppose that the pain of an act of sacrifice is in *itself*, as *pain*, pleasing to God; that, in giving up a pleasure or an indulgence or an easy life, the essential value of the sacrifice is the amount of suffering it costs us. Surely not. The suffering, however important an element it may be, is accidental. There are not a few who think that in proportion as they cease to feel the pain of some act of self-denial, it loses its value, and they often torture themselves with fear because they do not suffer more. When prayer or self-denial becomes a pleasure to them, they feel as if a good deal of their value was gone.

No doubt suffering has its own great and mysterious office as a means of purifying the soul, and as penance for sin, but that is a different thing. I am considering it now merely as an element in mortification and self-sacrifice, and the idea that it is *the* essential element upon which the value of any act of self-denial depends is assuredly non-Christian.

Yet again, the practice of mortification is not based upon the idea that the things we give up are in themselves bad. There has always been a tendency with some minds to regard certain things that have been abused by many people as in themselves evil. Everything in the world was created by God, and on the morning of creation, "God saw all the things He had made, and they were very good."[113] Those things that have caused the greatest evil upon earth are good and capable of doing good. The evil lies not in the things, but in the men who abuse them and become enslaved by them. The abuse of narcotics has been the curse and ruin of many a man's life, yet the proper use of them has saved many another. "The love of money is," says St. Paul, "the root of all evils,"[114] yet in the hands of a good man, money is an immense power for good.

[113] Gen. 1:31.
[114] Cf. 1 Tim. 6:10.

The Church has often been pressed to condemn things that have been the source of much evil and has been looked upon as lukewarm because she will not take the extreme view that is so often taken by those outside. But she has ever been firm in maintaining that "every creature of God is good, and nothing to be rejected that is received with thanksgiving, for it is sanctified by the Word of God and prayer."[115]

Therefore, in the practice of mortification, we do not condemn those things we give up. We do not throw the blame upon them, but upon ourselves. He who grows in the Christian spirit of mortification looks with no cold eye of contempt upon the fair world in which he lives; still less does he condemn those who use what he gives up. The condemnation he reserves for himself alone, and he regards with reverence those things from which he turns away. If there is in him any touch of bitterness or hardness, or any spirit of condemnation of those who enjoy what he has abandoned, we know that he has failed.

For the value of mortification is as a means to an end; it is the end that interprets and sanctifies the means. And the end is not death, but life. It is not the act of mortification in itself nor the pain that it costs that gives it its value, but what it gains. It is not the mere giving up but the receiving, the surrender of something good in itself for something better. The pain of the sacrifice is valuable as witness and test of the worth of that for which the sacrifice is made and the faith of him who makes it. It is a surrender of the lower for the higher, the dying to things less worth having to win things more costly.

[115] 1 Tim. 4:4-5.

The act of dying is but the passage into a larger life. We do not die for the sake of death, but as being the only way to break through the barriers that hold us back from a better and wider life. The martyrs have been known to sing *Te Deums* in the flames, and, on the rack, they caught glimpses of the life to which death was the short and painful passage, and it was on this that their eyes rested. Suffering was for them the condition of entering into the glory beyond, and they trod with kindling eye and outstretched hand that fiery passage, eager to seize upon the life to which it led. So St. Paul says of our Lord that, "having joy set before Him, He endured the Cross."[116] In the darkness He saw the light and reached toward it. In His Passion He pressed forward to the Resurrection.

∽

In mortification, focus on what you gain,
not on what you lose

We often dwell upon the act of sacrifice, upon the chill of a mortified life, upon the sternness of the demands of Christ, as if such acts ended in themselves. But we should look through and beyond them to that for which alone they are made and for which alone they are worth making, and see the pathway of death made radiant with the light of the life beyond.

Such an idea of mortification robs it of its gloom, and still more of all that charge of unreasonableness which is sometimes brought against it. We can gain nothing worth having in this world without paying for it. To acquire anything, however fragile and perishable, we must part with something we

[116] Heb. 12:2.

already possess, which we value less than that which we would acquire. If we do not think it worth the price, we do not pay it. The law of gaining possession is the parting with what we value less for what we value more. He would be unreasonable who thought only of the price he paid instead of the thing he purchased. Rather, he forgets his loss in the joy of his gain. It is the *possession* that his mind delights to dwell upon, rather than the cost. A man cannot keep his money and at the same time get what he has set his heart upon having. The question is which he values most. Our Lord says, "The kingdom of Heaven is like unto a treasure hidden in a field, which a man having found, hid it, and for joy thereof goeth and selleth all that he hath and buyeth that field."[117] The pain of parting with everything was lost and forgotten in the joy of his new possession. The predominant feeling was joy, not sorrow; gain, not loss. The pallor of death is lighted up with the glory of the life beyond. "Mortality is swallowed up by life."[118]

Such, then, is the principle of mortification taught by our Lord and exemplified in the lives of a vast multitude that no man can number.[119] It is in truth the carrying out of a natural law in the spiritual life. The saint is only doing in the higher sphere what is done every day in the marketplace. The principle is, "Little for little, much for much, and all for all." He who values this life more than the life beyond the grave will purchase its pleasures and enjoyments at the price of that life. He who believes that he was made for eternity, and that his home

[117] Matt. 13:44.
[118] Cf. 2 Cor. 5:4.
[119] Cf. Rev. 7:9.

and happiness are in that other world, will be ready to sacrifice this world for it. He who so believes and finds anything here on earth come between him and the life he has chosen will be ready, at whatever cost, to give it up. For the joy of the hidden treasure, he is ready to sell the field.

∞

Be ready to "die" to rise to
a higher state of life

But it is not always to the next world that we have to sacrifice this. There are ever rising before us here on earth worlds of higher possibilities than that in which we dwell. As the visions of such worlds rise before us and stir our hearts with the desire to enter into them, the law by which we enter is always the same. If we would rise into a world above us, we must sacrifice the one we dwell in. We cannot keep hold of this and at the same time rise up.

The boy looks into the great world of manhood and sees the larger life of those who dwell there, but he cannot enter into it until he dies to his boyhood and gives up its pleasures and its occupations and so passes on to the world above him, into which he has so long gazed, of which he has dreamed, and for which he has prepared himself. So the young man looks up out of a life of idleness and pleasure-seeking into the more strenuous life of thought and usefulness. He looks up and sees those who live in that higher world, he feels its attraction, and at the same time the strength of the bonds by which he is held in his present world. That higher world is all around him, appealing to him by its promise of better things, and its vision makes his low world of pleasure look very small and limited and poor, but he can pass into the higher only by the law of sacrifice and mortification.

He must seek the things of that world above him, set his affection upon it and mortify the members of his body that cling to and are entangled in that lower world in which he lives. If he cannot die to the old life, he cannot live to the new. It offers itself with all it has to give, but he must make his choice: live and die, exhausting his powers in the narrow life of pleasure, or dying upward into a life that opens out wider prospects and stirs his heart by more stimulating hopes.

Those who watch him as he passes into the new life see the meeting and blending of death and life, the death agony to the old, the birth pangs into the new. They see how truly life is the other side of death, the pain of breaking away from some old habit or association as the price of being able to enter into some keener enjoyment. "Mortality is swallowed up by life."

And these worlds of new promises and better hopes are always opening before us, calling us to enter and make our own the good things they have to give, but always upon the same condition: none can pass upward save by dying to the lower. We may live in the narrow world of self-centered egotism, measuring everyone and everything by the petty standard of their relation to us, and we may rise and pass upward into ever-widening spheres of thought and interest and activity, until self has been lost sight of in the crowding claims that press from all sides upon heart and brain.

How hard it is to rise. How fast each bond binds us to the lower life. How dim and impalpable the vision of the world above us until we enter in and take possession and how substantial the grip of those things for which we live, until, with pain and tears, we break away and die upward into the world above. Then how poor and shadowy and worthless the world we leave seems when looked at from above — like the toys of childhood seen by the eyes of a man.

So we pass onward and upward from the lowest to the highest edge of the kingdom of human nature, ever dying so that we may live more fully, the pathway of our life strewn with those things we once valued and cast away so that we might fill our hands with things more precious — the eye becoming more keen of vision to see the true value of things, the hand more sensitive to their touch.

But can we rise no higher? Is the limit of our natural power the limit of our possibilities? Are all our resources to be found within ourselves and the sphere of their activities in the world of men and things around us? No.

There are times when most men feel capacities for greater things than this world supplies: a possibility of knowledge and action that craves for a wider sphere than they can find here on earth, a power of love that cannot be satisfied. Like pinioned eagles, men beat against the bars of creation and wish to soar aloft to the infinite.

Having risen through one realm after another in the natural order, from a life of pleasure and self-indulgence to a life of thought and usefulness, man cannot rest. He would still press onward, break through the limitations of his own nature, and press his way upward into the kingdom that is above him — the kingdom of Heaven.

But how can he? Where can he find a lever to raise him above himself?

All that is human he can do, but within the limits of his nature lie the limits of his possibilities. The beast may develop instincts and intelligence that are almost human, but he cannot cross the barrier of his own kingdom. No more can man unaided enter into the kingdom of Heaven than the beast can enter the kingdom of human life or the inorganic can enter the world of organic life.

If he is to rise, he must be lifted across the barriers and placed within the realms of the heavenly city by the hands of One stronger than he, by a Citizen of Heaven.

In the first of all His parables, the parable of the sower,[120] our Lord taught, from the analogy of nature, the conditions under which such a passage from a lower kingdom to a higher was possible, and that it was the object of His coming on earth so to raise man.

The method by which man's transformation is effected does not stand alone, a startling exception to all God's ways wherever else they can be traced. On the contrary, there is a close analogy between God's method of working in the natural and the supernatural order. Our Lord bids us look and study in the workings of nature the methods of grace.

The silent, motionless, inorganic world finds itself in close relationship with another world, touching upon it, seemingly almost within its reach, yet infinitely separated from it: a kingdom of life and beauty rich with all the manifold variety of form and structure and color. There is a presence there that rules everywhere and transforms all that it touches. Into that kingdom it cannot force its way. It is shut down and held back

[120] Matt. 13:3-8.

by impassable barriers. It can push its way up into the heavens, or assume strange forms that mimic life, and, under the action of certain forces, it seems endowed almost with the attributes of life. It can press forward to the utmost limits of its own domain, as the sea beats upon the shore, but it cannot pass them.

The barrier between the inorganic and the organic cannot be broken through from below. There are points of approach where the two kingdoms seem almost to meet and blend, but upon examination, it is found that the gulf that divides them is really as wide as ever; they are separated by an infinite distance.

There is only one way by which the lower can cross the gulf and pass into the higher kingdom. If some visitor from the world above will descend and enter into the kingdom below and unite itself to it, taking the inorganic into itself and communicating to it the gift of its own life, and lifting it into the kingdom from which it has come. Only so can it rise. The power to rise is not in itself; it is communicated to it from another, one who has life. By union with that visitor from the world of life, lifeless matter can be made a partaker of its wondrous gift.

The seed descends into the earth, buries itself in its womb, takes into itself the elements that the earth supplies, makes them a part of itself, weaves them into the texture of the growing plant, lifts them across the hitherto impassable barrier, transplants them into another world, and, in transplanting, transforms.

Who could recognize the earth so transformed by the magic touch of life? Who could have guessed its latent possibilities that the seed has revealed? From the life that was in the seed, the organism of the flower has received its form, color, and structure, but the material of which it is made is taken from the lifeless earth.

Take it to pieces, and you will find nothing but what is of the lower kingdom of inorganic matter. The microscope can disclose nothing else, except that mysterious hidden presence which no eye has ever seen, which binds and fuses the various elements of earth in such wonderful combinations and harmonizes them into a complex unity.

From where does the glory of that fair flower come — the exquisite blending of its colors, the perfect molding of its petals and the sweet perfume that bathes it in an atmosphere of its own? It comes from the *life*. It is the crown of glory that life can set upon the dull brown earth if it yields itself into its hands.

As long as that presence, unseen yet vibrating through every atom, holds them together, they live and are partakers of the glory of the kingdom into which they have been transplanted. If it relaxes its grasp, they turn back toward the earth from which they came. When that presence is withdrawn, those wonderful combinations dissolve, their beauty pales and dies, the gates of death are opened so that these elements of the earth may pass back again into the inorganic kingdom from which they were lifted, and the powers of that higher kingdom are withdrawn forever. The earth rose through the gate of death, dying upward into a higher world in the grasp of the power into whose hands it yielded. It dies back again, through the death of decay, into the lower world from which it came.

Our Lord told His Apostles, "So is the kingdom of God, as if a man should cast seed into the earth."[121]

If man wishes to rise beyond the limits of his own nature and enter into the kingdom of God, he can rise only by the same laws as those by which inorganic matter can pass into the kingdom of life.

∞

Let Christ impart divine life to you

A visitor from the higher kingdom must descend into the lower, take into Himself the elements of which that lower kingdom is composed, making them His own, infusing into them His own life and holding them in its grasp, endowing them with His power, enriching them with His attributes, crowning them with His beauty, and penetrating them with His presence, and thus transplanting them into the kingdom from which He comes.

This was done once for all when "the Word who was with God and was God . . . was made flesh and dwelt among us";[122] when the King of that heavenly kingdom Himself came down and, uniting man's nature to Himself, lifted it across every barrier that had hitherto held it down, burst open the gates of death, and bore it in His mighty grasp to the very throne of God. And it is done for each one of us individually when, in Baptism, the Sower sows the seed of the incarnate life in our nature. Then there is imparted to each of us in our weakness a power that, working like a seed in the soil, can lift us up above

[121] Mark 4:26.
[122] John 1:1, 14.

the capacities of our own nature, making us, as St. Peter says, "partakers of the divine nature,"[123] and transplanting us from the kingdom of earth to the kingdom of Heaven, from the kingdom of nature to the kingdom of grace.

As the earth is powerless to rise until the seed, bringing a new and mysterious force into it, seizes upon those elements in it which yield themselves to its influence, and transforms and raises them, so it is with this divine seed cast into the soil of human nature. It enters as a new force into our nature, and there is absolutely no limit to the height to which it can raise it. It can "take the poor out of the dust and lift the beggar from the dunghill and set him amongst princes."[124]

As the earth becomes transformed under the molding force of the life in the seed so that it is scarcely recognizable, manifesting extraordinary powers and revealing possibilities that were unknown, so does man's nature under the forming and quickening powers of grace. It is the seed that reveals to the earth its latent powers, wakens them, and uses them. So does grace reveal man to himself. Coming into his nature, it shows him what he can be — new uses to which his powers can be put, new combinations, new developments. Like the seed in the soil, it draws under its influence various elements scattered through our nature that are seemingly useless and disconnected and weaves them all into a wondrous unity, seizing in its strong grasp all that can be laid hold of and taking it into its service. It can enable us to do things that by nature we could not do, showing us at once our own weakness and its power.

[123] 2 Pet. 1:4.
[124] Cf. Ps. 112:7-8 (RSV = Ps. 113:7-8).

And as the earth under the molding hand of the life that is in the seed reveals magical powers that transform it, so does man's nature as he yields to the forming and quickening powers of grace. It can be as different as the waving cornfield, ripe with its golden harvest, differs from the barren earth. Where that heavenly seed has been planted, all things become possible. The kingdom of Heaven, with all its riches, lies open to be entered and taken possession of: "All things are yours . . . and you are Christ's and Christ is God's."[125]

As the flower, in all its glory of color and beauty of form, is but matter under the new creative influence of life, so is it with man, newborn into the kingdom of God with the energy of the divine life acting within him. The material, if I may use such an expression, of the virtues of the saints is human; the creative force is divine. The elements out of which the noblest Christian virtues are formed are the elements taken from the earth of our poor human nature, but the molding force is in the seed "which is the Word of God."

∞

Surrender yourself to God's grace

But there is another law. The seed cannot act upon the earth unless the earth surrenders itself to it. In the parable of the sower, our Lord taught that the growth of the seed is entirely dependent upon the soil; if it is hard or rocky or thorny, it will prevent or mar its growth. If it is "good soil,"[126] yielding itself entirely to the action of the seed, it will bring forth fruit

[125] 1 Cor. 3:22-23.
[126] Cf. Matt. 13:8.

to perfection. The earth must surrender itself to the new force that has come down into it to raise it up; it cannot rise of itself, for it neither has the power nor knows the way into the kingdom of its new inheritance.

With man it is the same. All the efforts of his nature cannot enable him to do one act above his nature; all his intelligence, courage, and determination will not enable him to pass one step beyond into the kingdom of Heaven. "Flesh and blood cannot possess the kingdom of God."[127] This is the work of that new life, that transforming force which, like a seed, has been planted in him.

It is his work henceforth to remove every obstacle to the operation of this seed, to surrender himself and all his powers to its molding hand, to die out of the lower kingdom up into the higher kingdom, into which this gift would transplant him. Henceforth, his life must be one of mortification, dying that he may live, a yielding of nature to grace, a surrender of the things of earth to the powers of Heaven, a constant mingling of the sadness of earthly surrender with the divine gladness of heavenly attainment.

No doubt there were tears on the faces of many an Israelite on the night of their great deliverance. The ties and associations of four hundred years had to be broken. They had to go into a new world and to leave the old. But as the breath of the desert breathed upon their cheeks, as its wide spaces opened out before them and led them up to the Land of Promise, their tears would soon dry; their sorrow would be turned into joy.[128]

[127] 1 Cor. 15:50.
[128] Cf. John 16:20.

There is always a sense of loss at first in passing from a lower to a higher life, but the loss is soon forgotten in the gain: the games of childhood in the strenuous work of manhood, the joys of home in the claims and interests of the world. And no doubt the breaking with those things that hold us down to earth is painful. The restraints and customs of civilization are difficult for the savage, but when he is tamed and educated and civilized, he knows how great are his gains. And as we pass from the undeveloped and spiritually ignorant state of the citizens of the kingdom of earth and become citizens of the kingdom of Heaven, we enter into "the liberty of the glory of the children of God."[129] This is the mortification that the Christian life demands: the surrender of our whole selves to the new life that descends from above to sanctify and energize every power and faculty of our nature and fit us to enter into the Vision of God.

In such mortification there is no unreasonableness, for it is the very height of reason to sacrifice the lower to the higher, the ephemeral to that which is permanent. There is no gloom, however great the suffering, for he who so mortifies himself knows that he is on the road to eternal joy. And often, amid the sorrows of earth, he gets a foretaste of that peace which passeth all understanding.[130] There is no bitterness, for it is the act of divine love; it is done for God and in God. It springs from no hatred of self, no morbid contempt for the things of the world. It endows the soul with a divine tenderness so that, however hard it is upon itself, it is ever gentle toward others.

[129] Rom. 8:21.
[130] Phil. 4:7.

Sacrifice the good for what is better

In such a one we see first the conflict and then the reconciliation of life and death — death conquering one form of life and endowing the soul with another and a better; death the conqueror and the conquered: "That which is mortal is swallowed up by life."

Chapter Nine

∞

Persevere

∞

Life is the school of character. We are placed here to be formed for eternity. We come unformed and plastic into the midst of surroundings that have a singular power over us for good or evil. Each of us has latent gifts and powers and tendencies, and the forces of life act upon us, molding and shaping us by their strain and pressure.

So sensitively are we constituted that everything around us affects us: the air we breathe, the special place on earth we occupy, the people we come in contact with. You can tell something of a man's characteristics by his geographical position, whether he lives in the north or south, in the mountains or plains. The climate in which he lives and the character of the land in which he dwells have something to say as to the kind of a man he is. We are sensitive to all, plastic to the touch of everything in this wonderful world in which we are placed for our discipline and training.

As, wherever we go on earth, above us are ever the overarching heavens, whose influences affect everything we see, mingling with all, coloring all, making all nature smile or frown or weep as they will, so the heaven of God's presence ever bends over us and affects our whole view of life.

So let us persevere in such ways as we have been considering, or in any of those manifold ways in which God is wont to teach those who are in earnest. Let us be determined that we will not rest until we have penetrated through the many chambers and corridors, thronged with those strange forms that hurry hither and thither bringing news from without or carrying out orders from within, filling all with the noise and tumult of their activity — until we have forced our way through all this and entered into the presence chamber and lifted the veil and seen ourselves face-to-face.

Let us discipline all our powers of mind and body and allow no voice of inclination or passion ever to issue a command or assert authority until order has been restored throughout the whole kingdom of the soul, and there is but one ruler whose lightest word is law, and that ruler receives his commands from God.

Basil W. Maturin
(1847-1915)

∞

"Who can forget the wonderful preaching power of Fr. Maturin?" asked the good priest's fellow vicar. "Full of information and instruction, it held his hearers spellbound. . . . It was a voice in the wilderness, and if it came through human lips, yet it breathed the holiness of the sanctuary, and seemed to sound from Heaven itself."[131]

Basil William Maturin was one of ten children of a Tractarian clergyman in Ireland. Religion was central to the family's life. Three of Basil's brothers became clergymen, and two sisters became nuns. Basil initially intended to join the army, but his brother's death from scarlet fever and his own serious illness from the disease changed his outlook, and he decided to pursue Holy Orders in the Anglican Church.

In 1870, he was ordained a deacon and worked as a curate in Peterstow, Herefordshire. He was later ordained a priest, and his tireless work impressed his parishioners. In 1873, he entered the novitiate of the Society of St. John the Evangelist, an Anglican religious order, in the parish of Cowley, in Oxford.

[131] Maisie Ward, *Father Maturin: A Memoir* (London: Longmans, Green, and Co., 1920).

Although very happy at Cowley, he departed in 1876 for America, having been chosen to begin a mission in Philadelphia. There, as rector of St. Clement's Church, he drew many souls to the Episcopal Church, including many Quakers, who, if unable to hear his powerful sermons, would buy copies of them to read and discuss. "He abounded in humor and sympathy and intellectual vigor," wrote Maisie Ward, cofounder of Sheed and Ward publishing house. "To hear him preach was to be caught up and swept along by a torrent of ideas. . . . His words would go straight to the mind of the one who needed them."[132]

Through contact with so many and various people, he gained a knowledge and developed a sympathy that gave his words the power to go to the heart of people's problems. Like St. Thomas Aquinas and John Henry Newman, Fr. Maturin believed that he could convince others of the truth only by first showing that he understood their point of view, which he was able to do, because he saw so clearly into their minds.

But not only in preaching was he remarkable. With his deep sympathy, his psychological insight, and his keen discernment of character, Fr. Maturin had a profound gift for guiding souls, which is evident in his letters to those who appealed to his holy wisdom. In counseling souls, he emphasized fidelity to the duties of each person's position and state in life.

In obedience, but with sadness, Fr. Maturin left St. Clement's in 1888, when he was recalled to Oxford. A year later, he visited his society's house at Cape Town, South Africa, and on his return to England in 1890, he spent several years preaching

[132] Ibid.

missions and touching souls. But it was also a time of soul-searching, as he struggled with doubts about the Anglican Church and felt drawn to Roman Catholicism.

Finally, in 1897, he was received into the Catholic Church, and, after further studies in Rome, he was ordained a Catholic priest in 1898. Although he found it difficult to start afresh in middle age, he tried to receive the truth in the spirit of St. Paul, who embraced Christianity despite any conflict with what he had once held true. "All that cannot be reconciled with the new Truth must go," Fr. Maturin said, "but it goes, so to speak, of itself — it is pushed quietly aside without much of a jerk or a jar, in the splendid synthesis by which all gathers around the new, central, all-combining truth, and discloses its place and meaning."

In 1910, Fr. Maturin tried his vocation as a Benedictine at Downside Abbey, but found the life too strenuous at his age. In 1914, he was given the parish of the Holy Redeemer, in Chelsea and became chaplain of the undergraduates at Oxford. When World War I broke out, however, few students returned to the university, so Fr. Maturin decided to spend the Lenten term in the United States, where he had preached during Lent in 1913. Although this Lenten course in America was successful, it was his last. On his return to England aboard the Lusitania, a German U-boat sank the ship, and Fr. Maturin perished with more than a thousand other passengers.

"When his body was washed ashore," wrote Maisie Ward, "it was found without a life-belt, and it was believed that he had refused one, as there were not enough to go round. Survivors from the ship related that they saw him standing on the deck very pale, but perfectly calm, giving absolution to several passengers. As the last boat was lowered he handed in a little child, saying, 'Find its mother.' "[133]

Noble in life and in death, Fr. Maturin was tirelessly devoted to leading souls to Christ. "To be lit with the divine fire, to be united to the very life of Christ, Fr. Maturin saw as the goal and the meaning of each man's life."[134] Fr. Maturin's life was truly lit with divine fire, and from his preaching and spiritual direction poured forth divine fire that touched and transformed the hearts of countless others.

[133] Ibid.
[134] Ibid.

∞

Sophia Institute Press®